Praise for Young Bae

"A native of Seoul, South Korea, Young Bae's childhood reads like a painful chapter of *Oliver Twist.*"

—360 Magazine

"Young Bae…is the epitome of perseverance. She shares her story to inspire women to have faith in their journey."

—Urban Magazine

"From Seoul to NYC, Young Bae overcame it all."

—Sheen Magazine

Young is Blessed

Young is Blessed

Young Bae

with Brandon Deyette

PERMUTED PRESS

A PERMUTED PRESS BOOK
ISBN: 979-8-89565-398-2
ISBN (eBook): 979-8-89565-399-9

Young Is Blessed

Cover design by Cody Corcoran

This book, as well as any other Permuted Press publications, may be purchased in bulk quantities at a special discounted rate. Contact orders@permutedpress.com for more information.

All people, locations, events, and situations are portrayed to the best of the author's memory. While all of the events described are true, many names and identifying details have been changed to protect the privacy of the people involved.

PERMUTED
PRESS
Permuted Press
New York • Nashville
permutedpress.com

Published in the United States of America
1 2 3 4 5 6 7 8 9 10

To my Creator
for bestowing upon me countless blessings
and to the love of my life,
my son Niko.

TABLE OF CONTENTS

PREFACE

Considering I'm writing this book—which is solely about me—it might seem contradictory to admit this, but I've never been the type of woman to talk about herself. I've spent most of my life focused on survival, on getting through, on doing what needed to be done. But recounting all these stories, committing them to the page for the first time, has given me more understanding and healing than I ever could have imagined. It's like finally holding up a mirror and being able to see all the parts of myself—unfiltered, unhidden.

My fans know me as a funny, bold, no-nonsense tattoo artist who doesn't take shit from anyone. And yes, that's part of me. But it's only a glimpse. Very few people know what I've endured to become this version of myself. They don't know the years of abuse, the betrayals, the isolation, the constant shapeshifting I had to do to survive. They don't know the war zones I've lived through—both around me and inside me. So, I'm choosing now to tell the truth. My truth. Not for sympathy but in the hope that my story helps someone else survive their own—or better yet helps them stop surviving and start living.

Because the truth is nothing stays the same. The only constant in life is change. It's almost paradoxical, isn't it? Change is movement, chaos, disruption—and yet it's the one thing we can depend on. Every experience, every relationship, every betrayal, and every breakthrough reshapes us. We are never just one thing. We are constantly becoming.

I went from an abusive home to being completely alone in a foreign country to launching a successful tattoo business to landing a role on one of the highest-rated cable TV shows in the country—and I'm still not done. When I arrived in the United States in 2007, I had eighty-three dollars to my name and couldn't speak more than a few words of English. I didn't know the customs, didn't understand the slang, didn't have a safety net. But I had my faith in God. I had my tenacity. I had my creativity. And most of all, I had my right hand.

That might sound strange, but let me explain. My right hand is the one thing that has never failed me. When I was a little girl in South Korea being beaten by my father, it was my right hand that helped me escape through drawing, painting, sculpting. When everything around me felt chaotic and cruel, my hand created something else: safety, beauty, peace. When I was older and finally able to leave, it was my right hand that held that one-way ticket to America. My right hand gripped the only eighty-three dollars I had to my name. My right hand built my career one tattoo at a time. My right hand held the machine that inked the stories of pain and redemption into people's skin. It paid my bills. It opened doors. It turned scars into art. It gave me a future.

So, when I decided to get my first tattoo, I knew exactly what I wanted. I wanted something that would stay with me. Not just on my skin, but in my soul. I chose a phrase I had heard so many times growing up: "Till Death Do Us Part." Most people associate that phrase with marriage, with vows, with the idea of undying commitment to another person. But to me, those words meant something else entirely.

There is a certain irony in that phrase. "Till death do us part." It's a romantic idea—two people promising that no matter what happens, they will stay together until the end of their lives. But life doesn't always work that way. I know this. I've lived this. I've been through two marriages that didn't make it until death. What did we get instead? Arguments. Miscommunication. Different dreams. Different directions. Sometimes, we didn't even know why we were falling apart—we just were. People promise forever, but nothing on this earth is forever. Everything evolves, everything fades, and to expect permanence is to miss the point entirely.

What I've learned is that real love isn't about lasting forever. It's about showing up fully while it lasts. No rules, no timelines, no cages. Just truth. And in my life, the only thing that has shown up for me consistently, unconditionally, no matter what, is my right hand. That's who I got married to. That's who I committed to. That's who I promised to honor till death do us part.

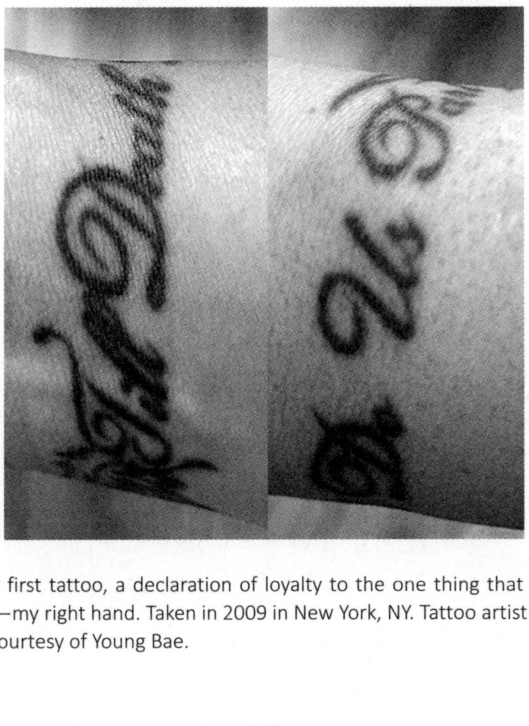

This is my first tattoo, a declaration of loyalty to the one thing that has never failed me—my right hand. Taken in 2009 in New York, NY. Tattoo artist: Elizabeth Markov. Courtesy of Young Bae.

Tattooing came into my life like a calling. It was everything I loved—art, expression, connection—wrapped up in one intimate act. The skin became my canvas. Every line, every shade, every stroke was a collaboration between me and the person trusting me with their story. What I love most about tattooing is the freedom. You get to declare who you are and what matters to you—publicly, permanently. That's why my first tattoo wasn't for someone else. It was for me. A declaration that I would always honor what got me here. My art. My strength. My right hand.

While I understand the majority of my story will come as a shock to many of you reading, it will come as an even bigger shock to people who have known me all my life. To all of you, this is my confession: what you read in this book may be surprising, considering you had no idea I sheltered everyone in my life from what was really happening at home. It may be a lot to process, but know that my intention was never to keep anything from anyone—I just knew what my status was in Korea and there was no way of changing that. The only way I knew how to survive the chaos of my home life was to recontextualize it. If the world around me wasn't what I wanted, I simply changed the way I saw it. Even now, in telling this story, I've had to decide how to share it in a way that honors both the truth and the privacy of others—so for their protection, I've changed some names.

Growing up, I learned how to mask my pain. I told stories to hide the truth. I crafted narratives to protect myself and the people around me. I wasn't trying to lie; I was trying to survive. I was trying to rewrite a life that felt too ugly to look at directly. I imagined a better version of my world, and I let art carry me there. I painted it. I dreamed it. I sketched it into existence. That was the gift and the curse: I could ink something beautiful from even the darkest chaos. But underneath it all, the truth still pulsed like blood beneath the skin.

That's what this book is about. Not just the story of a woman who escaped her past. Not just a timeline of struggle and success. But a story of a woman who created her own reality—one drawing, one tattoo, and one bold choice at a time. A woman who made a sacred promise to herself and kept it. A woman who has been beaten down, abandoned, overlooked, and underestimated—and is still here. Not because she was saved, but because she saved herself.

So no, this isn't just a story of overcoming. It's a story of becoming. It's a story about love—real love—the kind you give yourself when no one else knows how. This is about faith, power, and art as salvation. This is about a woman and her right hand.

This is our story.

This is how we survived.

This is how we thrived.

This is how we will never go backwards.

This is our journey—Till Death Do Us Part.

아...
씨발
힘들다..

CHAPTER 1

THE UNSETTLING AWARENESS OF YOUR HEARTBEAT

Throughout my life, I always had feelings I never quite knew how to express. I couldn't laugh when things were funny or cry when I was sad, because showing emotion only led to more punishment. If I cried after getting beat, my dad would beat me again for crying. So the only safe way I found to release any of it was through creating art. It was my way of expressing what I was experiencing inside, especially when I couldn't find a word to associate with that feeling.

I was just three years old here, drawing in my mother's art studio while she taught other children in the room. Taken in 1988 in Seoul, South Korea. Courtesy of Jungok Kim.

I remember looking up to my older sister and thinking how cool she was, that I wanted to protect her or be her, and I just wanted to be around her all the time. The feeling was not mutual, but that is the burden of being the younger sibling. Still, I couldn't quite put into words the feeling I had. It wasn't until I was much older that I realized the feeling I had for her was love.

Love.

How fucked up is it that I didn't know what the word "love" meant? I had heard of it. I had been told the definition, but I wasn't entirely sure what it was. To me, love was an unwavering and unconditional feeling that you put into action, demonstrating the emotion with words of affection, tenderness, hugs, kisses, protection, loyalty, and not causing harm.

This isn't to say I never received any kind of love from my parents—they just never said it. I never heard the word come out of their mouths. And if they did show me love, they just didn't show it the way you would anticipate love to be shown. I guess this just stems from my parents never understanding what unconditional love was, so by default, they couldn't show me what it was like to truly love and be loved.

There are two things I have in common with my mother: we are both artists, and we are both the black sheep of our family. My mother was born into a wealthy, prestigious, artistic family. My grandfather was a famous Korean photographer known for his images of the Korean War and for ushering in commercial photography to Seoul in the 1960s. His work is well renowned and is on display in numerous museums throughout the world. My mother, Jung-Ok Kim, followed in her father's footsteps to become an artist. So how does Daddy's little protégé become the black sheep? Simple: she married my father.

My mom's wedding day. This was the moment she unknowingly gave up everything for a man who would take more than he ever gave. Taken in 1979 in Seoul, South Korea. Courtesy of Jungok Kim.

There are also two things I have in common with my father: his stubbornness and his DNA. That's all we have in common, and that's all we will ever have in common. I know at one point my father was probably charming, charismatic, maybe even romantic. He did somehow sweep my mother off her feet. I have seen some love letters my father had written to my mother when they began dating. Cute, but I wouldn't fall for that shit. Maybe I'm too jaded now, but if my entire family is against me marrying someone, and my friends are too, they may have a point. If the man you're about to marry is accessorized in red flags from head to toe, it's probably a sign you should bail.

After my grandfather cut off my mother financially from the family, she continued to pursue her career as an artist. I honestly have no idea what my father did, but I don't remember him ever doing much. We always joked about him coming from a family of grifters and scammers; essentially that's what they did—they scammed people. And he certainly scammed my mother into giving up everything in order to be with him. When I say everything, I mean everything: her money, family, sanity, future, and career. Her life.

My parents were married in the late '70s, and in 1980 my older sister, *unnie* was born. The two of us couldn't be any more different. At least in my mother's eyes, my sister was the pretty, smart one. She was the favorite. And it wasn't a secret either. My mother made it very well known that she was.

That's me in a bikini when I was three, already considered the chubby one in the family. Taken in 1986 in Seoul, South Korea. Courtesy of Jungok Kim.

In fact, most people didn't even know I existed—or at least that's how I felt when I was around my mom and my sister together. My mother barely acknowledged I was alive, and my sister enjoyed that. She mocked me for it; she knew what my mom was doing and enjoyed the shit out of it. I was the rebellious, artistic, and—according to my mother—chubby one. Highly unfavored.

Not to mention my mother's side of the family had barely anything to do with us, which just left me with the Bae Scammer Family. And while I was closer to them than anyone else, we still weren't close.

Before I was born, my parents were barely getting by financially with my sister. My mother had rented a studio where she taught art in the front, and in the back was a curtain that separated the studio from where my parents and sister slept on the floor. No furniture, just some blankets and a floor. That's it. My father would allegedly work odd jobs every now and then, but it was my mother who was the real breadwinner. She kept the roof over their heads and put food in their bellies. And she never asked for any help—not from her family, not from anyone. Because she knew she wasn't going to get it. It would be an embarrassment not only to her but to her entire family.

One thing you need to know about Korea—at least in my own experience—is that poor people don't exist. Like they exist in the fact that there are poor people, but Koreans don't acknowledge their existence. In Korea, there's a deep shame tied to poverty; it's seen as a personal failure, not a societal issue. Unlike in the United States where people might still find pride or identity in the hustle regardless of their income level, Korea values image, education, and status to such a high degree that falling outside those norms makes you invisible. It's not just about having money; it's about maintaining the appearance that you do. So, we played the part even when we had nothing.

My family never talked about being poor—my mother was too proud to admit anything like this. And beyond pride, we knew that if we were honest about our situation—whether it was poverty or abuse at home—we'd just be judged, and our lives would've been even harder in Korea. She worked hard, took financial care of her family, and busted her ass enough to lead people to believe that she and my father were doing better than they were actually doing.

Like perhaps that they had an actual apartment to live in and were not sleeping on the floor in the back of an art studio. That's the picture they painted to the world.

I was born on October 9, 1984, in Seoul, South Korea—and I was technically a surprise. My mom knew she was pregnant, of course—it wasn't like one of those TV shows where a woman thinks she has food poisoning and ends up giving birth in a hotel bathtub. She knew I was coming. But what she didn't expect was that I'd be a girl. During her pregnancy, she prayed every day for a son. She even took ancient Korean herbs believed to help conceive a boy. She spoke to me in the womb, calling me her little boy. She was certain. It was supposed to be one girl—my older sister—and one boy—me. So when I came out a girl, it was a bit of a disappointment—I even heard stories that she cried out loud. But that feeling didn't last long. She took one look at this chubby little face of mine and couldn't help but fall for me.

Things were pretty rough growing up in Korea. And I'm not being dramatic. I know a lot of people have lived in challenging conditions, dealt with so many horrors, and I'm not here to negate that. Our struggles are different, but there is a common thread amongst all our collective stories: in the face of adversity, you have a choice to either succumb to it or rise above. My family teetered on that thin line between the two. We never had enough money. We bounced around from place to place. One studio for another, one shithole for another, one less bed available to sleep on. Terrible living conditions, verbal, physical, and mental abuse, and, above all else, a lack of emotional support came with it.

I don't have many memories from before I was four years old (or five, if we're counting the Korean way, where you're considered one year old at birth). Don't ask me why because I don't know the answer. I just accept it like a lot of things that have happened in my life. But some things I just can't accept. The way my father treated us is one of those things.

One day, around that time, he came home and was on one. He was yelling and screaming at my mother. I don't remember if he hit her or not, but it wouldn't surprise me if he did. But I do remember him walking toward my sister, the rage in his eyes. This was in the back area of my mother's art studio, behind a wall she had constructed to create a separate living area for us—a small back room where we could cook, sleep, and do everything else. It was no more than eight feet wide and six feet deep. This was what we called home, where the four of us lived and slept on the floor.

This fear, anger, uncontrollable seething rage came over me. And in that moment, everything fell silent. Each move was slow and deliberate, a pause between each breath. There was a stillness in the room. I could hear and feel the rhythm of my heart beating. And it became louder, quicker, heavier. As he approached my sister, I became defensive.

You will never hurt the people I love. Never!

My sister was sitting on her knees on the floor, wringing her hands over and over, her whole body trembling. Repeatedly crying out, "I'm sorry," again and again, like a broken record. She just sat there automatic, defenseless.

But not me. Without thinking, I charged at him with all my four-year-old might. I would force him to stop before he could lay a hand on my sister.

In an instant I was airborne, soaring across the room. I landed with my back against the wall, hard enough to leave an indent—something that was normal in our home, where holes and dents in the walls were just part of the scenery. My head was swimming and throbbing, and my back was aching as I tried to regain consciousness.

Because I loved my sister, I had to try to help. I didn't know how to articulate it, but I loved her so much. What was my mother doing? She was doing the same thing she always did. She was trying to stop my father, and in the process, she got beaten up as well.

I could see him standing there, hovering over my sister. But I had become so trained, so desensitized, so numb that all this seemed normal, so every day:

Wake.

Wash.

Eat. Or maybe not eat.

We get beaten.

School.

Hide.

Fear coming home—or is it home?

Maybe we can eat again; I'm not certain. But I am certain he will beat Mom again, and I'm certain he will beat me again.

Maybe not today. Today may not be my turn. There was this constant unsettling feeling, never quite knowing what will happen today, tonight, or when I wake up.

But every time he's there, he's looming over us, beating down our pride, our joy, our lives, our dreams. He beats them down, hitting and pushing them further and deeper until I stare at my dreams from my corner of the barren, freezing studio…or is it sweltering hot? I can't tell, but inside me it's cold. I don't cry. I don't react. I don't feel. I just look beyond my dreams and the blood, the bruises, the fists, the shame, and the pain…and I feel nothing. Nothing at all. *One day I will feel something,* I tell myself. *One day I'll have a real home. A place where he can't follow.*

But that day hadn't come yet, and the worst was still waiting for me—and it was coming fast.

CHAPTER 2

SILVER LINING ON A GREY CLOUD

There is nothing worse than being poor in South Korea except for people knowing you are poor.

And we. Were. Poor.

But no one really knew. My friends didn't know, my parents' friends didn't know, and my sister's friends didn't know. But because of school documents, my teachers always knew. And they treated me accordingly.

Before I was five, my memories come in pieces, mostly just getting beaten by my dad, or us sleeping on the floor of our makeshift living space. It wasn't until I started school that concrete memories started to form. I remember that it was around that age we stopped regularly attending church. Catholic church.

Most Koreans aren't religiously affiliated, however almost 30 percent are Christian, with a third of those being Catholic. That was us, though we certainly didn't live in a very Christian home. Flipped tables, shattered glasses, food flying across the room. Fists raining down in rage, beating me senseless. Rinse and repeat every day. Not very Christ-like.

But if we were going to fool society into thinking we weren't poor, we had to put on airs. Show up to church on Sunday in our best clothes, our best hair. Hide the dirt stains, blood stains, bruises, and scars—though not so much bruises and scars, because he usually hit us where it wouldn't show, where it could be easily covered up. Smile and nod. No one was the wiser. Except, again, the teachers.

At school in Korea, our teachers knew each family's income—mainly because your name would be on a list to get free lunch or some kind of similar aid for low-income families. You could always spot the rich kids by the way they carried themselves. In elementary school, my mom managed to hide our situation well enough that no one really asked questions. But even before I stepped into a classroom, I already knew my family was different, and not just because all the other families had houses or apartments and beds to sleep in. It was that they ate dinner together every night without drama. They just ate and talked, like civilized human beings.

As a family, we also ate together every night, but it was mostly out of fear. And every night, we didn't know which version of my father we would get. Would this be a night of simple conversation? Or just the sounds of food cooking on the *bapsang* table, chopsticks lightly tapping on our plates, and the barely audible chewing through the dead silence? Or will this rice bowl, along with the rest of the dishes, fly past my head, careening across the room until it hits the wall and floor, which my mom will have to clean up—but only after we get our asses beaten?

Who knows? No one ever did. And it's not like there was anything in particular we did or said that would set him off. It just happened. And while we didn't get beaten up every day, we lived in fear daily. That was the reality throughout my entire family life in Korea. I wish there was a reason. Like if he were an alcoholic, or a drug addict, had a gambling problem, or something else that could have explained his erratic behavior. But nope, there was no such reason.

Abuse is something that happened almost on a daily basis during my childhood. It's hard to completely understand what that's like and what it does to your psyche if you haven't lived in that specific situation. You can be empathetic towards survivors and victims of abuse, but unless you've experienced it, it's hard to wrap your head around the deleterious effects that last a lifetime.

But I didn't know it at the time. I wasn't aware of what abuse was—I thought it was normal. It wasn't until one day in Korea, when I went to a friend's house and ended up staying a little too long, that I realized it wasn't normal. Her dad came home from work carrying a bag of snacks in one hand and bungeo-ppang, a fish-shaped, red-bean paste pastry, in the other. As soon as he walked through the door, my friend and her two siblings ran to him screaming, "Daddy!"—jumping, hugging, fighting each other just to get kisses and his attention. He was smiling from ear to ear, laughing and talking with them. I remember just standing there, completely shocked, because that was the first time I ever saw what a family was supposed to look like. I always thought scenes like that on TV were made up—some fake shit. Later, after I moved to the United States and slowly began to open up a little and told people what I went through, that was the first time the concept of abuse was ever really brought to my attention.

Let me give you an example of a typical day in our household that involved some form of abuse. Korean culture requires you to remove your shoes when you enter a house. It is a sign of respect to do so. Our homes are sacred to us, and we treat the ground with dignity. We eat sitting on the ground, we sleep on the ground, and we keep it as clean as possible, sweeping and scrubbing the floor by hand every day. Always barefoot inside. No shoes. Which makes this story a little infuriating.

This didn't just happen once. This happened often. I would be painting or drawing, my mother cooking or cleaning, my sister just existing and being an annoying older sister, and my father would enter the house. Slowly, he'd pace around. You could tell when he was about to get upset, and really anything could make him upset. It didn't take much—he'd say something, anything, like "How's school?" As soon as he opened his mouth, it was like a trap—I knew we were in trouble. We would begin to answer, and he'd start getting angry for no real reason. He would grab whatever was closest to him (a glass, a plate, a bowl—anything) and either throw it at one of us, at the wall, or on the ground, where it would shatter into hundreds of tiny pieces. He would begin to yell and scream, often about nothing, just anger. He'd start accusing my mother of not allowing him to fulfill his dreams; he would berate us for being stupid; he would blame us for all his failures in life. And if we'd show any sign of fear, anger, sorrow, or any emotion whatsoever, that's when he'd lay into us. That's why, whenever I was home with him, I'd tiptoe around, hiding in corners, doing everything I could to avoid giving him a reason to open his mouth in the first place.

My mother, my sister, and I would be on our knees in total submission and cowering in fear.

He'd break and destroy things that mattered to us—knowing we couldn't afford to replace them. Sometimes he'd even ruin the little food we had, which we could barely afford in the first place. That was just as damaging—maybe even more so—because it tore us up mentally and emotionally. Open-hand smacking across the face, over and over. Throwing objects at us. Beating us until he was tired and walked away. But he didn't walk away all the time. And in those moments, we hoped and prayed that he would leave so we could cry in peace—or just breathe. Usually, he would stay while we suppressed our sorrow, because the sound of us crying would warrant another round of beatings.

To have this happen once in your life is devastating. To have this happen almost every time we were in his presence is so mind-boggling that it's difficult to really assess what kind of emotional, psychological, and physical damage he has done to us over our entire lives.

And after the violent storm would settle, we'd be left to clean up the mess. All the broken pieces on the floor. Tiny glass shards scattered around the room.

But oddly enough, we got good at cleaning up these messes. It was almost like a routine. But that's the biggest problem: it had become so normalized to us that we had figured out a routine. The quickest, easiest, and most efficient way to clean up fractured, miniscule slivers of broken glass from the floor. If that's not fucked up, I don't know what is. But we got good at it; I'd say we pretty much became experts. Because if we missed just one tiny piece of glass on the floor, chances were that within a day, we'd be picking out shards from the bottoms of our feet. Which was a painful physical reminder of what we had just endured.

Sometimes I felt like that was our punishment even after we were beaten. Even if all the pieces of glass were cleaned up, our every move in the house was like walking on broken glass. Every step I took was a psychologically painful reminder of the very thing I tried to erase from my brain on a daily basis.

From time to time, my father would find himself with a piece of broken glass in his foot, which he would blame us for and inevitably we would have to pull it out for him. The irony didn't go unnoticed. When he wasn't around, it was perhaps the only levity we had in the situation—the ability to laugh at how his actions ended up hurting him as well. Not even he was safe from his own rampages.

We had just moved to Mok-dong, and I remember thinking this would finally be the place where our lives got better. Taken in 1991 in Seoul, South Korea. Courtesy of Jungok Kim.

Being home was shitty, but do you know what's even worse than going home to a shitty house where you never know what's going to happen? Going to a shitty school where you never know what's going to happen.

Yeah, remember those teachers who knew I was poor? Well, they certainly made sure I knew about it every day. Back then in

South Korea, money ruled everything. It ruled how people treated you, how society viewed you, and how your worth was determined. And I wasn't about to allow my parents' current financial situation to have any effect upon me or my life. At least, not at my core.

Teachers of poor kids can get away with anything, including beating kids. What, you think the teachers would get in trouble? Or that I could just bring this up to the school administration? Hell no.

I learned that lesson early—like in elementary school, when I was sitting at my desk doing my work and a few classmates nearby started whispering. I said one thing to them—just one—and the teacher saw me talking. Only me. So what did they do? They called me up to the front of the class, holding a large, thick stick. They'd ask, "How many times do you want to get hit?" And I'd pretend to think about it and say, "One?"—hoping to make it easier. But then they'd start yelling, "How many times?"—pushing back and forth until finally they just decided on their own, hitting me as many times as they felt like. I'd return to my seat with a deep bruise on the back of my thigh, trying not to show how much it hurt.

That kind of thing happened all the time for no reason. Whether it was a slap, a wooden stick, or something else, teachers felt entitled to lay their hands on us whenever they wanted. And I'm pretty sure I got it worse because I was poor. They knew I wouldn't say anything. I was an easy target.

I wouldn't talk about this with anyone. I never thought about asking somebody for help. I didn't know if "help" even existed. Maybe it did, but I didn't know because of how I was raised. I had no clue. I just knew since I was little that I was on my own.

You think I'm going to risk asking for help only for my parents to find out, then have them be embarrassed by my actions followed by a guaranteed ass whooping from my father when I got home? I never brought school problems home. And I never brought my home problems to school. I always took care of things on my own.

Plus, the teachers didn't want to deal with my parents either. My parents were never called to come to my school even though I got in trouble from time to time. Instead, those teachers beat my ass for any reason they could possibly think of, to set an example for the rest of the kids, to show me they had authority, to remind me I was poor, or for no real reason. They just knew they could beat me without any consequences because they knew if I opened my mouth, I was on my own.

Another reason the school probably never contacted my parents was because I told them that my dad was dead. No one ever asked how he died. Everyone only ever saw my mom come by the school, so my secret was safe. He was never going to show up, and they were never going to come to my house. To most of the teachers at my school, my father was dead—and as far as I was concerned, he may as well have been.

I didn't know what emotional abuse was. All I knew was that my teachers beat me, and my friends' mothers didn't want them to hang out with me. I must have seemed bad or dressed differently, or my clothes weren't brand-new. I couldn't talk to anyone about what was going on at home nor what was happening with my teachers. I just sucked it up. And perhaps that resolve was what got me through all the troublesome days, the uncertainty, the volatility.

That and my art. Art was always my escape. I don't remember when I started painting or drawing; I just remember I always did it. I never had to learn; it was inherent within me. Perhaps I absorbed a lot from living in my mother's art studio, seeing all her students doing art projects. But I believe it's in my DNA, perhaps from my mother, who is an incredible artist in her own right. Or my famous grandfather. Either way, everyone saw my talent from an early age.

When new families would come into the studio to speak with my mother about classes for their kids, I would already be sitting up front drawing and painting because it was what I loved to do. My mother never forced me, and in fact if she had, I probably would have lost interest. I hated being told what to do. So, she would treat me as if I were a student she taught.

This was me painting at the front of our studio, where my mom used to pretend I was her student to help drum up business. Taken in 1986 in Seoul, South Korea. Courtesy of Jungok Kim.

"She's so talented!"

"Oh, yes, she's been my student for many years," my mom would boast.

Excuse me, ma'am. I'm your daughter.

And then she'd go off on a sales pitch about teaching me and showing the progress I've made in her class—as if my creations were the result of hours of her training and teaching me everything I knew. It worked because they saw what I could do and wanted their kids to draw like me. They bought right into it, and my mom didn't have to say anything else. We knew how to hustle.

Little did they know, this "art studio" was actually our home, and behind that makeshift door in the back was where we lived. We didn't have a shower or a bath. We washed in a small basin. We ate at a small *bapsang* table. We slept on the floor. We also didn't have a toilet inside our home. Outside of the studio by the staircase was a creepy communal toilet. I used to hate going there, especially at night. At times, out of fear, I would find a corner of the art studio, and I would poop there instead. When my mother would discover it in the morning, she would be so pissed. Luckily, she always assumed it was one of her students, not me.

I played along with the idea that I was one of her students. I pretended she was just my teacher, and the parents gushed over my work. No one was the wiser. It was at this point, around five years old, that I have my first memories of people praising me for my art. And it worked—pretending to be the protégé student kept business flowing. So much so that within two years, my mother had saved up enough money to get us our own apartment—this time in Mok-dong, a middle-class area of Seoul. I wasn't quite certain what to expect. We were promised a better, happier life.

We would have our own bedroom to share, just my sister and me. It sounded too good to be true.

But wait, did this mean we wouldn't be sleeping on the floor in the back of my mother's art studio? Did this mean I could escape into another room and avoid complete contact with my father? Was this...a silver lining? I was just as dubious as I was excited about the prospect of this new start.

As my fantasy world was being built in my mind, behind the scenes a new terror was on its way to destroy the very hopes and dreams that served as the foundation for my potentially perfect and exciting life.

내가 표현을 안하는 성격이지만 엄마가 마음속으로는
내 속을 알고있었으면 좋겠어서 이렇게 쓴다 엄마...
엄마 내가 말 안하지만 엄마를 항상 대단하다고 생각하고
있어.. 또 이렇게 건강해서 고마워... 나도 엄마 하고 싶은거
다 하게 해줄려면 시간이 필요하잖아... ㅋㅋㅋ 엄마가 아프면
큰일이잖아 그치...? 그니까 항상 건강하게만 살아줘 엄마..
나 진짜 엄마의 은혜에... 사랑에... 보답하고 싶어.
엄마 집 가지고 그림 그리며 살고 싶다고 했잖아. 내가 하게
해줄게 엄마. 알았지? 곧 사줄께.
내 말 믿지? 엄마 나 허풍쟁이 아닌거 알지?
ㅋㅋㅋ 그러니까 항상 웃으며 건강하게 살고있어.
엄마 절대 우울해 하지말고... 엄마 친구들 부러워 하지마.
엄마 딸보다 돈 잘버는 딸 가진 사람 없어.
엄마 알지도 못하면서 우울해하지마 ㅋㅋ 엄마딸이 최고로
성공했어. 그리고 나는 점점 더 멋진 사람이 될꺼야
엄마가 다 가르쳐줬잖아. 어떻게 힘든 상황 헤쳐가는지
어떻게 하면 거지같은 상황에서도 희망을 잃지 않는지...
엄마가 나한테 다 가르쳐주고 엄마는 까먹은거 같어 ㅋㅋ
엄마 걱정하지마.. 걱정하면서 살지마..
엄마의 최고의 작품 "내가" 있잖아.
특히 돈 걱정 하지마... 알았지?
엄마는 최고의 엄마야.. 나한테는 엄마가 최고야!!!
알았지? 사랑하고 존경해 엄마 ~ ♡

- 엄마의 마스터 피스
영롱!!! -

7/29/2014

CHAPTER 3

As If It Never Happened

In the late 1970s and throughout the 1980s, there was a rather peculiar and fucked-up trend happening with Korean children of poor families. Parents who no longer could provide for their children, offer them a better life, or just didn't want them would take their children out to a restaurant. They would dress up their children in their best outfits, cleaned and nicely pressed clothes, with their hair washed and well-groomed or styled, and go out for an expensive and often really good quality meal. Their last meal together.

The parents, or often a single mother, would order their kids food—then halfway through the meal, the parents would excuse themselves from the table and never return. Just completely abandon their children. Most would hope that someone rich or a couple who couldn't have kids would take them and provide a better life. Everyone knew about this. We'd hear people talking about it all the time and see it on TV dramas or movies. I'm not entirely certain what became of those children, but I can only imagine they ended up in orphanages, foster care, or on the streets. It was harrowing as a child to watch these stories and to hear people talk about it. Especially since we too were suffering and poor. It was like looking into a mirror and seeing myself in these kids, which was probably the reason for my paranoia. I was always scared my mom would leave us. Not because she didn't want us but because I couldn't find a reason why she should stay in this shithole with us. Whenever I'd see these TV dramas and movies, that feeling would come up inside me—this anxiety that gripped me with fear.

Before we moved to Mok-dong, my mother surprised me with a mommy-daughter lunch date. Just the two of us. Not my dad. Not my sister. I washed myself up, brushed my hair really pretty, and put on one of my best outfits. Just me and my mommy.

We arrived at the restaurant, which was *Gwangyang* style, and I thought to myself, *I know this place*! *This is the place we ate that creamy soup I love*! My mother ordered my meal, starting off with the creamy hot soup. As excited as I was, there was an air of uncertainty about what was going on.

My soup arrived, and my mother excused herself. She told me, "Keep eating. I'll be back soon." I sat there staring at the soup, nervously wondering what would happen next. And this rush of anxiety washed over me. Was I about to be like those poor children I saw in Korean dramas or movies? I thought to myself, *I should've been a better daughter to her. If she comes back, I'm never going to make her worry about me again. Never*! *Just come back, Mommy*!

I shoveled the thick soup into my mouth, not even hungry but forcing myself to eat while smiling so no one would suspect what was happening. All the while, my stomach was churning and felt like it was tying itself into a knot.

A while passed, still no Mom. The server came out with my main course, donkkaseu pork cutlet with brown sauce, a side of white rice, and shredded raw cabbage. I remember putting the food in my mouth, chewing, and swallowing. To the outside world, I was acting fine like I always did. Inside I was holding back my tears and my fear. Everything else was blank. Time sort of slowed down, and all I could focus on was trying not to make anyone notice what was going on. I sat there for what felt like an eternity. I don't know if I ate more, or if I just sat there. After a while, the waiter stopped coming by to check on me.

Three hours later, Mom showed up. I was just so ecstatic that she came back for me. She grabbed me, and we left. We didn't speak about it. No discussion. Ever. It's as if nothing happened.

It was the first time I had felt like, *Damn, this could really happen to me! Is she going to leave me?* At the same time, I couldn't understand why she hadn't left us. Because in my little head, I reasoned that if I were an adult, I definitely would have left. I told myself that she probably went to take care of some business really quickly, and she left me at my favorite restaurant, so I didn't have to follow her around. It was totally normal for kids to be alone in Korea, but that's not what my anxiety told me at that moment. I was just living in constant chaos and fear every day. My biggest fear, even at six years old, was that one day my mom would leave. I mean, that was partially my paranoia speaking, but deep down I also knew her life could have been so much better without us kids around.

My mom and I at the studio—just before I realized even the moments that looked picture-perfect were built on unstable ground. Taken in 1987 in Seoul, South Korea. Courtesy of Jungok Kim.

I always felt unsettled, uneasy. This prompted me to start really hiding my feelings and my pain, my problems at school, just everything in general. I didn't want to burden anyone, especially my mother, with my thoughts. I just wanted her to feel better about her life, so she wouldn't leave us—so she wouldn't leave me.

Like I said, at this point in my life my mother had saved up enough money to buy our own place. We moved out of our makeshift art studio to Mok-dong. At the time when we moved, it was three years after the 1988 Summer Olympics. The area had boomed to accommodate housing for the Olympics. Even though it was a middle-class area, there was still a lot of affordable housing available. My mother took the opportunity to snatch up one of those apartments, and we moved into a two-bedroom place that had an actual bathtub.

While we finally had our own apartment and not an art studio, it was a lot smaller to me. I was used to having the whole art studio as my "house" after the students went home for the day, my own indoor playground to run around and play in by myself. This new apartment felt restrictive and offered less personal freedom.

I remember walking into our new place, and there was an area to put away your shoes, as is customary in all Korean houses. It opened up to a dining area connected to the living room, which had a balcony and a small kitchen off to the right. To the left was the bedroom my sister and I shared. Yes, we had our own bedroom—but still no beds. We did have two *bapsang* tables, long and rectangular, that we laid a stack of blankets on to create cushioning. Under our makeshift beds we had our clothes and belongings. And there were two tiny desks between our beds where we did our homework, where I painted and drew.

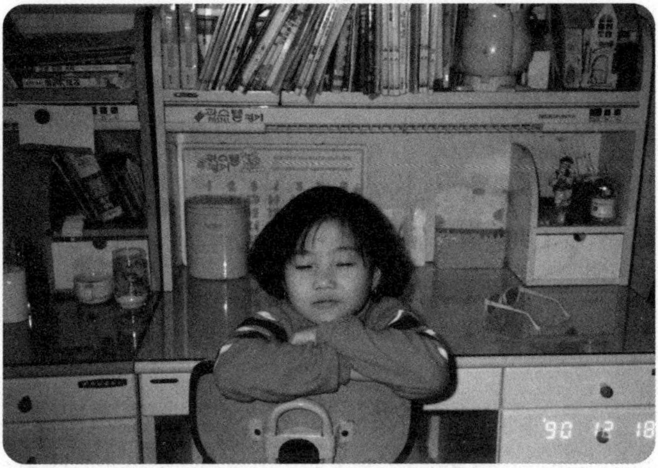

This is me sitting at my desk at our first real house, before everything changed again. Taken in 1990 in Seoul, South Korea. Courtesy of Jungok Kim.

Between our room and my parents' master bedroom, which also didn't have a bed because they just slept on the floor, was the bathroom. It had a toilet, sink, and yes, a bathtub. To have a real-life bathtub had been beyond my wildest dreams—and don't get me started on having a toilet that wasn't communal. It was actually in our apartment!

I had my hopes up that things would change. And they did for a short while. For the first time in my life that I can remember, my father landed a job, with *Time* magazine. I'm not certain what he did, but he had a business card that had the *Time* logo on it. We were all excited for two reasons: for one, this meant he was out of the house during the day Monday through Saturday; and two, this gave us hope for the future, and we were finally moving up in the world. My mother was so proud of him and so were my sister and I. I remember him telling my mother about the next steps in life and how this was going to make everything better for our family.

Now and then, he would even bring home various magazines that were a part of the *Time* magazine family.

This is when I discovered fashion. I can still feel the excitement bubbling up inside of me when he'd arrive home with new magazines in his hand. I would sit there for hours staring at the models, the clothing, the styles. And I'd start drawing my own versions that I came up with in my head. I had hope.

Sadly, my hopes were just that. After about nine months, somehow, he lost his job. No clue how, and we certainly didn't ask.

Before and after school I was usually alone; this was my free time. I got to do whatever I wanted. Usually, I'd come home after school and just paint and draw. Other days I'd wander the streets. And some days I'd stop by one of the corner stores and steal shit. I did it for the hell of it. Didn't matter what I would take. Candy, drinks, anything really. I mean, it's not like I had money to pay for it anyhow. So, I'd just steal it.

This went on for months until one day, I was in the store browsing through the aisles, looking for a nice, sweet treat to enjoy on my walk home. I grabbed some candy and went to place it in my pocket.

All of a sudden, this old man comes careening down the aisle toward me, screaming in my face. I will never forget the look he had—pure rage—or the bitter and furious way he cursed me out. He made me write my name, address, and phone number to alert my parents. Of course, I wrote down all the wrong information. I didn't want him to come around to my house. It was at this moment when I realized that my actions could potentially cause worry for my mother. I felt scared, nauseated, defeated. Mostly I felt guilty. This horrible, acidic feeling in the pit of my stomach ached with embarrassment. Just thinking about how disappointed my mom would be if she ever found out was enough to make me sick.

But my parents never knew. They really didn't know much about my life outside of our apartment.

In the afternoon, I would enjoy my little walks through town on my way home from school. I'd pass through parks and playgrounds, making sure to play on each one before returning home. I would get home, drop off my bag, pull out some paper, and just start drawing clothes inspired by the magazines that my father brought home. I was fascinated with fashion: dresses, skirts, shoes, anything. That was my outlet. Living in this world on paper and escaping into my future, I wanted to dress like those models I would see. Fashion and drawing clothing designs, to me, were a way to express my individuality, creativity, and passion.

I'd spend hours making designs, sketching ideas, and passing the time before my father would return home. Because we all knew that when he was home, we didn't know what was going to happen next.

Even with my father's temporary, short-lived success, he still treated us the same. He just had fewer opportunities to flip out on us because he actually had to work now. He would still fight with my mother constantly about money and about his family. His family was like, "Oh, you bought an apartment. You must have money now, and you're not sharing." That kind of hustler shit. Because that's who the Baes are: hustlers. But in reality, we were barely making ends meet.

My father has three older brothers, one older sister, and one younger sister, all of whom are grifters themselves. The oldest brother kept to himself mostly. He would, on a few occasions, show up drunk to my mother's father's house. Yes, this is my father's brother—no relation whatsoever to my mother's father. There was no reason why he would. Just drunk. Which is a big taboo in Korea. For one, my grandfather Kim was a very famous and rich man. My uncle was not. And two, you don't just show up to people's houses unannounced or uninvited. These occasions would cause my grandfather to call my mother and chew her ass out. Which then would cause my mom to berate my father, which would then cause my father to beat the shit out of us. So thanks, Uncle, for being a drunk and causing me to get beat.

The second-oldest brother had one eye. The other was fake. I don't know much about him, but he was nice to me. I remember he had these toes that looked like they were melted. Some people said it was due to a drug addiction, and others said he was on medication from being sick when he was younger that caused his toes to be deformed. I don't know if those were just rumors or if they were true; no one confirmed, and I never asked.

His older sister was the scary one. She was beautiful and charismatic, but she always had a look in her eyes that said, "I can kill you." I don't know how to explain that feeling, but when you meet someone like that, you just know if they had to, they would. Her husband was allegedly *kkangpae,* which is organized crime—like *yakuza* or mafia. When she met her husband, he allegedly kidnapped her for several months, and when she emerged, they got married. Probably Stockholm syndrome, who knows?

His third older brother was in and out of prison for various reasons. He was the type of guy who believed he owned the world. Whatever anyone else had, in his mind, it was his. The most preposterous scam, possibly my favorite he allegedly did, was he somehow sold a mountain to a group of people. Like, he sold an entire mountain that he didn't even own. How cunning and manipulative do you have to be to pull that off? I couldn't make this shit up if I tried.

The youngest sister was my favorite of his siblings. She was cool, fashionable, funny—she was actually quite kind to our family.

The Bae family was close-knit and family-oriented; they cooked great meals, laughed constantly, and fought just as often. But don't cross any of them because if anyone messes with their family, they will fuck you up.

So here is their brother, married to the daughter of a famous photographer; they just bought a new apartment in Mok-dong, and he's not sharing any of the wealth with his own family? Yeah, they were pissed because they felt they deserved a piece—if not all—of the pie.

And because they were pissed, my father was pissed. And because he was pissed, we got beat. Nothing had really changed since we moved to Mok-dong. I really thought things were going to be different. The first time my father acted crazy in our first real apartment, I just felt disappointed. I really thought he was going to change. But it was just a new place, same old bullshit. Everything was pretty much the same except now we had a bathtub and a toilet.

My mother taught her art classes in our living room, making money off our neighbors who wanted their children to draw just like me.

Most days when I got home from school, I was the only one home. During the school week, my mother would run errands until early evening when she'd come home to teach class—and on weekends, too. I relished that alone time, because when my family was home, I had to be quiet and reserved. Outside of home, I could be loud, vibrant, and whomever I wanted—and when I was home alone, I could be the same way. I'd walk into the house and just start creating art, and I didn't have to pay attention to anyone else.

In our apartment building there were fifteen floors, and every floor had about six apartments. The stairwell going up to each floor and the hallways leading to the apartments were exposed to the outside in an open-air design. This allowed the tenants to leave their smelly trash outside their front doors until they felt like taking it downstairs to the dumpster. The halls would be just lined with full trash bags.

Out of boredom, I suppose, or even just being a mischievous child, I would grab the trash bags from in front of their apartments and start throwing them over the edge onto the ground below. I would begin at the top floor and work my way down to the fifth floor. Every floor, every apartment, every trash bag. Why did I stop at the fifth floor? Because I suspected people could see me from the fourth floor and below. I was running a covert operation, and I couldn't allow my identity to be revealed. I didn't do this daily, just whenever I felt the need to purge the smelly hallways.

The neighbors were incensed, and they ended up holding a community meeting to deal with the problem of trash all over the sidewalks and the parking lot. Imagine if one of those bags had hit someone below? No one had any idea that it was me. I was the shy, cute girl. I was inconspicuous.

If I wasn't painting, drawing, or tossing the neighbors' garbage, I would generally wander through the house, being nosy. I would look for notes that my mother had left behind. She was really into writing notes, just random ones—mostly her thoughts or reminders to herself. I liked reading these because it gave me insight into what she was thinking or feeling. I loved reading them because they were a part of her, and it made me feel like I had her to myself for just that moment.

One day while enjoying my solitude, my sister came home early. When she entered our room, she had a note in her hand. With a blank expression, she handed me the note. The letter was from my mother. She wrote to us to explain she decided to leave for a week to go to a *gidowon,* a retreat prayer center. No other explanation—she just went. I stared at the letter as tears began to well up in my eyes. My heart dropped. *Did she finally give up? Could I have been a better daughter?*

I couldn't breathe. Tears were streaming down my face as I sobbed inconsolably. My sister just stood there and stared at me. I was confused, sad, and hurt. She offered no consolation, which I wasn't expecting from her. We weren't the consoling type of family. And to be fair, she really didn't know what was going on in my head—and I wasn't about to tell her even if it helped explain my reaction.

When my father got home, my sister gave him the note. I was so scared he was going to beat us for whatever reason. My feelings of pain and hurt turned into fear and worry. But you know the weirdest thing? He didn't. In fact, during the entire time my mother was gone, I don't remember him hitting us at all. Which was probably the longest stretch of time in my childhood that my father did not inflict physical violence on anyone. And that made me upset because why couldn't he be like this when my mom was there?

Why had he been acting crazy all these years? Was this what caused my mom to leave? I was just so upset and hurt that my mom left. I thought that might've been it, like she was just gone. I was so sad, but of course I didn't show it.

About a week later, my mother showed up. No explanation, no discussion, nothing. She just walked into the house and acted like she had been there the whole time. It was just back to normal for her, as if it never happened.

It was *always* back to normal, as if it never happened. And we carried on, rinse and repeat.

Right as I was finishing the third grade, my mother decided it was time for an upgrade again. She decided to sell our apartment in Mok-dong and move out east to the suburbs of Gyeonggi-do, about an hour and a half outside the city. The apartment in Mok-dong had gone up in value, and with the profit from selling it, we could afford an even better place in the suburbs.

And there it was again: hope. Hope that at the next place things would get better. I couldn't have been more wrong. What seemed to be a golden bridge to a better life was really a trap door to the gates of hell. And everything I had ever known up until that point would eventually just wash away.

As if it never happened.

CHAPTER 4

It All Falls Down

Change never bothered me. I was always excited for something new. A new place, a new adventure—change was good. It also left room for hope, and my hopes were still high.

For most kids, moving to a new school causes so much uneasiness, but I didn't look at it that way. I was just excited to get to meet new friends, explore new areas, and start fresh in a new place. I felt like I could just erase all the fucked-up stuff out of my life and start all over again.

Even though Gyeonggi-do was considered the suburbs, it wasn't like the suburbs in America. It was more like an extension of Seoul, a sprawl of the mega city. It still looked a lot like where we lived before, crowded and busy, just farther from the city center. But for us, the move promised a better life: bigger space, better schools, and the hope of a fresh start.

Our new place was all I had hoped for, with three bedrooms, and one of those was my own. Now I had my own room to escape to when I needed it.

Not every day was horrible. There were some good memories sprinkled in here and there. However, those memories start off nice and generally take a turn for the worse.

One day my father surprised me by suggesting we go out for a bike ride together. I was ecstatic. Just my daddy and me. For all my father's faults and the anger I had toward him, I truly loved him. I didn't know what love really was, and I didn't know what it meant, but that's how I felt. I mean, he is my father, after all. Deep down, all I wanted was for my father to show me love back. But that excitement I was feeling quickly turned to apprehension, remembering *I never know what's going to happen.*

At our new apartment in Ilsan, a new city in Gyeonggi-do, our complex was connected to a large park that spanned our neighborhood. I used the bike my aunt had given to me because my cousin had outgrown it. My father used my sister's brand-new bike.

We brought our bikes down the elevator to the first floor. My dad took the lead and began to pedal down the path leading from the apartment complex through the park. I followed right behind him. Not even thirty seconds into our bike ride, I watched my father stumble, the pedal whacking him on the back of his ankle. I immediately came to a halt.

I closed my eyes, and I could feel my heart beating so fast, pumping blood directly to my face. Panic.

Oh, shit. I'm dead!

He glared at me. I didn't make eye contact. My apprehension turned directly into fear when out of the corner of my eye I could see him mouth to me, "You fucking bitch." Then he picked up my sister's bike and headed back inside.

I didn't know what to say. I didn't know how to calm him down, so I shut up. I feared anything I said would be used against me. I grabbed my bike and walked it inside to the elevator.

I cautiously entered behind my father into the apartment as he screamed and cursed. My mother and sister, acting overly concerned, inquired as to what had happened. This further infuriated my father. My mother ran to get some peroxide and ointment to take care of his "injury." He put on this whole theatrical show about how badly he was hurt, and how it was my fault.

First of all, it was a tiny scratch on the back of his ankle. Second, how was it my fault that he stumbled? My mother and sister babied him, hoping to spare us from his usual tantrum. But that didn't work. He continued to blame me for what happened, as though I somehow caused this. I began to speak up to defend myself, but then I just stopped. I realized it didn't matter because he was going to explode anyhow. And he did, throwing glasses around the room, shattering them against the walls and on the floor.

With him, every good memory is tethered to a shitty ending. So, I locked it all away. All the anger, pain, and even the little bit of happiness. It was how I coped. Put up this wall and keep it all inside. Away from my family, away from everyone. I yearned to leave my house, to go outside into the world where I could be free from it all. I could act as if nothing happened and just be by myself. *And one day when I'm older and away from all of this,* I vowed, *I will always speak my truth and never hold it inside.*

Until then, every day was tough. And it only got tougher as time went by. I kept quiet. And I didn't let anyone in. I learned to compartmentalize my feelings. I learned when the going gets tough, I keep it all to myself. I learned how to press forward. But I never learned how to heal. I only learned how to shut everyone out and protect myself. That's how I coped. And my art. That's how I survived. This was how I functioned.

But even in this new space, the emotional rollercoaster of living with my father remained. The walls might have changed, but the fear lingered. And yet, sometimes—just sometimes—we laughed. That's how we survived.

We moved toward the end of the school year with only three weeks remaining of the third grade. Korean school begins every year in March and ends in February. We got one week off in the spring, about two months off in the summer, and another month off for the winter. I had barely made an impression at my new school before we had an entire month off prior to returning the following school year. At least I had Mari to keep me company. She was the best dog ever, a white Maltese that we got right before we moved.

My mother made flyers promoting her art classes with our phone number typed vertically at the bottom, so interested people could tear it off and call her for teaching. She and I would post the flyers up around the neighborhood, placing them on individual building community boards. This worked well enough to attract some new students, but Koreans typically spend their money sending their children to *hagwon* academies after school for additional studies, plus sports activities. Korean kids stay busy. At-home art tutoring isn't known for being a huge money maker in Korea, but my mom did the best she could to put food on the table and a roof over our heads. Money was always tight.

I started the new school year—fourth grade—walking myself to and from school. Now we lived closer, just a five-minute walk compared to the twenty-minute hike I used to take in Mok-dong. Fourth grade wasn't anything special. I made some new friends, but nothing everlasting. Except Jieun—although we didn't become close until sixth grade—which turned out to be convenient because she lived in the same apartment complex as me in Ilsan. From the outside, we were just like everyone else. We were normal. It wasn't better or worse than my old school in Mok-dong—it was just different. A new life, a new routine. The next year, in my fifth-grade class, I met my other best friend, Jaeyong, and we instantly hit it off. They've been my ride or dies ever since.

Around the same time, like always, my mother found another opportunity for us. She discovered an apartment about fifteen minutes away by bus in a slightly nicer part of the city. It was cheaper than the mortgage she was paying on the apartment she bought. She found a tenant to lease our apartment for a year and charged him more than the mortgage. With the extra rent and the money she earned teaching art classes, she was able to cover both the mortgage and the rent on a new place.

We moved again, just down the road, into a four-bedroom apartment with two bathrooms; it was the biggest place we had ever lived. The fourth room became my father's private space, which he filled with books, old American magazines he had saved from his short time working at *Time* magazine, and stacks of LaserDiscs.

If you don't remember LaserDiscs or are too young to even know what they are, they're like the predecessor of DVDs but the size of a record. Huge monstrosities that took up too much space. One little scratch and that LaserDisc was done for. Same with fingerprints. While my mother was busting her ass trying to save up money, pay our mortgage, and put food on the table, he's out there spending her money on stupid shit like LaserDiscs. Building up his collection to boost his pride because it made my father feel like he had money that he could show off. To the outside world, my father had it all.

New place, same old shit. My mother found new art students. I traveled farther to school, and my sister still ignored me. And of course, my father still couldn't hold down a job. At times, he did land jobs temporarily. But inevitably, he lost the jobs or—oddly enough in a lot of circumstances—the companies would go out of business. No matter how large the companies were, somehow just him showing up was a part of their eventual demise.

When we first moved into the place, the landlord met us in the parking lot to let us into our new apartment. She was unloading paint buckets out of the back of her car to bring up to the building. My father, being the ever-helpful man that he was to everyone but us, offered to assist her bringing up all five paint buckets. Big, strong man.

Only the weight of these buckets, with their thin metal handles, started digging into my father's hands. As he was carrying them across the parking lot, up the elevator, and into the house, we could see his anger building up inside him, ready to explode. But the landlord was with us, so he had to play it cool.

As soon as she left, my father went off—yelling and screaming at us, throwing things around, all because he hurt himself by helping out someone else.

Tensions began to rise even more than usual at home. I didn't quite understand why, considering we were living in a nicer place. One time, I remember my mother finally arguing back with my father. This had never happened before. I was only ten years old, but I can distinctly remember finally understanding what was happening, what they were arguing about, and what was about to go down—and it all had to do with the Bae Scammer Family.

Back then in Korea, they made it almost impossible for a woman to own property by charging them excessive amounts of taxes, making them jump through hoops in order to have property without the husband's name being on the title. Typical Korean patriarchal bullshit. My mother did like every good Korean wife is expected to do, which is to put her husband's name on the title that she rightfully purchased herself. Which meant that the property was also in his name, not just my mother's.

It seems my father's oldest sister, the one married to the *kkangpae,* had convinced him of a great way to get them out of debt. By giving her a $150,000 loan against the apartment, she would then flip the money in a susu club. In this proposed arrangement, everyone would pay into one pool, and as new people were added, the original people would cash out their money, eventually doubling what they put in. She agreed to pay the monthly bank loan until it was paid back in full, all the interest made while in the bank would go to my father, and there would be extra money on top of it for him to get us out of debt. In my father's eyes, it was foolproof.

This plan was in response to covering another loan he had already taken out for his youngest sister for $20,000. Yes, he had already taken out another loan against the apartment—on which his other sister defaulted. And he never told my mother.

My mother didn't see it his way at all, and they argued. This time, my mother fought back. All the years she worked so hard putting her blood, sweat, and tears into busting her ass every day teaching these kids in her studio, so she could save up enough of her own, hard-earned money to buy this apartment. She was furious. She finally argued back, defending herself, which I hadn't ever seen happen—so this was a big deal. And she still got beat for it. There was nothing she could do. My father had made up his mind, and that was the end of any discussion.

Before the start of our summer holiday in the middle of fifth grade, my mother surprised us by saying she was taking us on a trip to Europe.

Wait, I thought we were poor? How the fuck are we going to Europe?

Apparently, when she sold the apartment in Mok-dong, she had stashed a little aside for emergencies—or, in this case, a family vacation. I always felt this was her way of saying "Fuck it." She already knew things were going downhill, and it was only a matter of time before she was going to lose it all. Plus, she didn't want the Bae family to get ahold of it.

We had gone on day trips around Korea, which inevitably ended up with my father getting mad and beating us at some point—in the car or when we got home, never in public—but we'd never traveled this far. Regardless of what had happened in the past, I was just excited about this new adventure. Because you know me, I like new things. I was really going to Europe!

Let me preface this by reminding you that to the outside world, my father was amazing. No one saw his behavior behind the scenes. Because we would be staying with family friends on our trip, this meant that the likelihood of us being spared from his tantrums was actually pretty high.

We arrived in England to meet up with one of his old Korean friends. He tried to impress everyone with the minimal English he knew. I don't remember much about the trip other than actually having a good time.

I remember going to Buckingham Palace and seeing the changing of the guards; you know the guys in the red suits and the fuzzy black hats. My dad had me on his shoulders parading me around London to show the world just how awesome of a dad he was. Looking back, it was all smoke and mirrors.

After England, we joined a big tour group and made our way over to France, saw the Eiffel Tower and the Louvre, and then we somehow ended up in Belgium. The only thing I recall about Belgium was my parents decided to take us out for McDonald's, which was a treat for us, period. We walked inside, and to my mother's shock, it was way more expensive than even the fanciest restaurants in Korea. I always found that odd.

We went through Switzerland and eventually ended up in Venice. Italy was super weird for me as all the Italians wanted to take pictures with me and touch my hair as if seeing a little Korean girl was unheard of, and they had to get photos. "*Bella, bella*," they'd say as they pointed at me, smiled, and waved. Nothing bad, just lots of attention. However, that wasn't what made this portion of the trip so memorable.

It was baked ziti.

Now, I'd had pasta before—spaghetti with tomato sauce. This was different.

What the hell was this shit?

And the way it looked reminded me so much of Korean *tteok* (rice cakes): thick, chewy, sticky. It looked exactly like *tteokbokki*, that sweet, spicy, chewy dish we were all dying to have after going weeks without Korean food. Koreans pretty much have to eat Korean food every day, so seeing something that looked like *tteokbokki* had us beyond excited. But then we bit into it, and it was cold, mushy, and had no taste at all. We were crushed.

I'd leave that part of my trip out when telling my friends back home—just skipped right over it.

For the record, though, I love Italian food now.

Overall, I remember the experience as a happy one. There were occasional times where my father would yell at us behind closed doors, but for the most part we pretended to be a normal and happy family.

When we arrived home, my mother stopped by our old apartment to check in on the tenant as his lease was almost up. To her surprise, he handed my mother a bag full of old mail of ours that he had been collecting for quite some time. Letter after letter, notice after notice—defaulted loans dating back months.

My aunts had only paid on the loans for a few months before defaulting on them. Yes, those same loans that my father took out against our apartment for his sisters. Suddenly, we no longer had any money. The tenant was moving out, so we had no way to pay for our new apartment. Our old apartment was about to be in foreclosure, and we were barely making ends meet as it was.

Saying that we were fucked is an understatement.

My mother got rid of our four-bedroom apartment across town, and we moved back into our old place that the tenant vacated. While our house was in the process of foreclosure, we hadn't been forced to leave the premises—yet.

It was a somber moment walking back into that old apartment. Sometime between returning from our trip and our tenant moving out, the bank had come around and placed red stickers on all items that had any value to be put up for auction, all over the entire apartment. My *bapsang* makeshift bed? Red sticker. My tiny desk? Red sticker. All the furniture? Red stickers. Everywhere.

But did we leave? Hell fucking no. We squatted there for an entire year. Yes, we lived there for an entire year with these damned red stickers on everything. Hiding out, avoiding anyone who knocked on our door, and cautiously looking out the keyhole of the front door to make sure no one was around when we left the apartment.

Every day, we were harassed by someone. Phone calls. Letters. People coming by our house. People trying to break into our house through the little milk hole that is at the bottom of every Korean door. (It's this circular hole with a flap over it, kind of like a cat door, only it's for milk men to put bottles inside your house instead of leaving them outside. Or for small packages. Or in this case, people with sticks trying to unlock the front door from the inside.)

The banks were hitting us hard and harassing us every day. And it wasn't just the banks that were coming by. Apparently, my father's oldest sister not only defaulted on the bank loan, but she bailed out of the susu club—so now the *kkangpae* were looking for their money, too.

We were fucked.

One day during this time, I was sitting in our apartment, enjoying a moment alone. I went to the bathroom and noticed some spotting of blood on my panties. I was so embarrassed. I panicked, tried to clean out the blood from my underwear. I washed it, blew on it to dry faster, did everything I could possibly do to try to clean out the spotting.

It wasn't that I was completely clueless as to what was going on. My parents never discussed it with me, but we'd learned a bit in school—though it was extremely biological in nature. Boys and girls go through puberty, girls have a period, and you should not engage in intercourse until you are married. Pretty straightforward and an extremely misguided approach to sex education.

After about two days, I finally told my mother what had happened. When I explained what was going on, she paused, went outside, and came back in with a rose in her hand. She sat me down and told me what this meant for me. Then she presented me with the rose—a symbol of my womanhood. It was mine, and I should protect it. She told me that I was now a "real" woman, no longer a kid, and I was able to have babies. Meanwhile, I'm thirteen and barely able to wrap my head around what is happening in my world, let alone worry about babies! She gave me pads and told me I needed to wear these every month.

Oddly enough, it wasn't until six or seven months after this that I finally started getting my period regularly. I now had a burden to carry: watch how I talk, how I act, how I present myself to the world, so I don't get harassed or even pregnant. Such a fucked-up thing to put the onus on a young girl to "act right" around boys because I could be harassed or get pregnant. As if they can't control themselves, and I have to adjust my personality from being who I am to a more subdued version of myself—fuck that.

After about nine months of squatting—and knowing our eviction was only a matter of time—my mother used what little remained of her secret savings to put my sister and me up in an officetel. These are office-hotel studios with mini kitchens, typically rented out to people traveling for business—not two young, homeless girls. To keep us safe, my mother would drop us off there at night and return in the morning. My sister and I lived there for about two to three months until my mother ran out of money.

Our apartment ended up going to auction and was sold. Even though we had received countless letters, phone calls, and even in-person visits from the authorities ordering us to vacate the premises, my mother and father held on tightly to the apartment as best they could. Avoiding the door, sneaking in and out even more diligently than before, keeping a low profile.

It was my father's hubris that was their inevitable undoing. One day, the new owner showed up to the door and offered a deal for my father to open it for her. In return, she would give him money up-front, so we could move into a new place and start fresh. I have no idea how they convinced him, but he agreed and opened the door, ready to receive a wad of cash and be on his merry way.

Nope! They just kicked his ass out. The new owner called the cops, and he was forced to leave. He lost his mind, and we lost everything. And with that, we were officially homeless.

We managed to grab most of our stuff, but not all our stuff made it. The bank took the furniture to sell at auction along with other valuable items. Over time, we lost a portion of our belongings little by little, every time we packed up and moved. An old family photograph, my precious fashion magazines, all my sketchbooks with my fashion designs.

It was a very confusing time with so much happening all at once. I went with the flow since I didn't have time to process what was going on.

We left Gyeonggi-do and traveled to Paju in the countryside, winding up at a town hall community center. Unknown to me at the time, this was where we would lay our heads for the next several days. Sleeping on the floor, clueless as to what would happen next.

In the morning, we were woken up by people coming into the community center for their daily activities. Laying there on the ground, I watched feet pass by my head as people shuffled around. My mother would take us into town every day, drop us off for school, set up a rendezvous time and place to be picked up later, then back to the country.

According to my friends, however, we moved to a big house way out in the country. Huge house. Bigger than they had seen.

My faith had always been strong, knowing that God had my back, and one day I would be free from all this shit. But hope was slipping away as the reality sunk in that we were homeless.

After a few weeks of living like this, we had to find a real place to live. Just as we were leaving the community center, an angel appeared. Not like an angel in the Bible with wings and a halo but a man who would eventually become a good friend of the family. He overheard our situation and offered our family a place to stay for a few months just so we could get out of the community center and hopefully get our feet back on the ground.

The catch was that it was a remodeled shipping container in the middle of the country.

It was a small countryside community with a few old houses. Our shipping container wasn't like any old container—ours had been gutted and refurbished. It's sort of hard to explain, but for a shipping container, it was pretty pimp. You walked inside, and it had an open area with a kitchenette, a refrigerator, and an area in the living room where my parents would sleep. There was a door that separated the main area from the back room that my sister and I shared. On the opposite end, there was an attached bathroom, which was an add-on to the original shipping container. It was separated by a sliding glass door, so basically you could see into the bathroom through the glass. There was a laundry machine, a toilet, and a shower area that just had a shower wand. Basically, we could see each other in the bathroom at all times. There I was, a teenaged girl with no privacy, just using the bathroom and showering for all to see. It wasn't the greatest, but it was way better than being at the community center full-time.

During the school week, we would travel about an hour each way from the shipping container to my school through the farmland and over the mountains into the city. I'm not a country girl, so I loved coming to the city. It also meant I was away from my father for a good portion of the day. Before we would meet up every evening to head back to the countryside, I would wander around enjoying the temporary freedom I had before I had to see him again.

By this point, I was in my second year of middle school, thirteen years old, and living in a shipping container about forty-five minutes away from my school and my friends. We would get up early every morning, travel back to the area where our school was, go to class, and then meander around after school for several hours until it was time to meet my mother at our designated meeting place and time. Then we'd head back to the shipping container. Sometimes, I would sit where I was supposed to meet her for hours. My sister would typically arrive right at the meeting time, so I'd be there alone just waiting.

After school, I'd either roam around being mischievous as usual, or I would go over, usually uninvited, to my friends' houses. I'd stay until it was time to leave, or it was apparent I was no longer welcome to be there. I couldn't go to Jieun's house all the time anymore because she started going to the *hagwon*, or a private academy, after school to further her studies. Jaeyong started to hang out with a different crowd for a bit, so a lot of the time I was left by myself.

By this time, between 1997 to 1998, pretty much everyone had a cell phone. Even my mother had one. But unlike all the other kids in school, I did not. I still had to use the phone booth to get ahold of my mother after school to confirm our pickup spot and time.

One day, I called her up to find out where we needed to meet up. She told me that she was teaching late and that I should take the bus back home to the shipping container. But since there weren't any direct buses, I would have to take such and such bus to get home, then get off after the second military base. Then she gave me instructions where to meet her by the bus stop where she would pick me up, and she hung up.

I hopped on the bus and nervously headed out into the country solo. I'm a city girl, and I hadn't spent much time out in the country. We passed by large farms and a few military bases. I didn't know which base it was—if it was the second or the third that had passed by—so I just assumed it was my correct stop. I got off the bus, fully expecting or at least hoping to see my mother. Nothing. Just me. The only one in the world out there in the middle of nowhere. I found a phone booth and called my mom's cell. Ringing, but no answer. Voicemail. I tried again. Three more times until I ran out of money. Since I didn't have any more money to call my mother, I had no clue what to do next.

I decided to wait. I waited and waited. After about forty minutes I decided she wasn't showing up. I thought, *I might know my way home from here.*

I started to walk. No distinguishing landmarks, just countryside, farms, and some houses scattered amongst the fields. I was in the middle of nowhere.

When I say I'm a city girl, I mean it. Living in Seoul, and even in Gyeonggi-do, was like living in Manhattan all my life. It was like all of a sudden dropping me off in the middle of Nebraska saying, "Find your way home." I can navigate public transportation, run confidently around city streets, and still figure out my way through a city. But country? Nope, I was scared and lost.

After about an hour and a half of wandering around the countryside, several trucks had driven by and still no sign of a neighborhood. All of a sudden, a truck pulls up next to me.

I'm freaking the fuck out! My guard is up, and I'm thinking, *Oh, shit—they're going to abduct me?* I pull myself together and acknowledge the truck.

The man rolls down the window and says, "Are you lost?"

I look inside and notice a woman, who nods at me with a smile. "Me? No, I'm fine. I know this neighborhood."

As if insisting I knew the neighborhood, which I didn't, would somehow throw them off from knowing I was, in fact, lost. Regardless, they drove off, and I kept walking.

From afar, I noticed a commemorative statue. It was the kind that has historical information on the plaque in front along with the name of the town you are in. I thought, *Hey, I remember seeing this near the shipping container*! *I found my way home*!

I followed in the direction of the statue, walking along the side of the road and passing through farmland. I walked for what seemed like forever. The sun was starting to set, but in the distance, I could see the statue. I walked through the fields and closer to the road until I came to an impasse. A ditch separated the field and the road, and it stood between me and the statue. It didn't look too big to get across. It had water running through it, and I had no idea how deep. There were also bushes that were in the way.

So, I charged toward the ditch, full speed, leaping in the air, aiming to land on the other side.

Fuck!

I barely missed the other side and hit the bank wall, falling back into the water in the ditch. I knew I was scraped up, covered in garbage that flowed in the ditch water, including pieces of barbed wire, but I had to pull myself out and walk toward the statue. Laughing in pain, my legs and hands were dripping wet. I climbed up the side of the ditch and onto the road. I walked over to the statue and read the placard.

Fuck!

This wasn't the right place. I walked even more, trying to find identifiable landmarks out in bumblefuck nowhere, hoping to see something that would point me in the right direction to get home.

When it started getting dark, I got scared. There were no streetlights to illuminate my way. It began to get colder as well, like really cold. I would have been warm, considering I was wearing my gym pants under my school uniform, but my pants were wet from falling in the ditch.

In the distance I saw a truck approaching. Again, I was not looking to get abducted, so I pulled myself together and walked as normally as possible. The truck pulled up, and it was the same guy with the woman. He rolled down the window and said he was out delivering things, saw me again, and figured he'd offer me a ride.

I looked at the woman in the passenger seat. I smiled and said I was fine. She smiled at me, and he assured me that I would be safe with them.

Inside my head I said, *Fuck it*. I finally admitted to them I was lost. I decided to risk everything and get in this truck with two adult strangers. I hopped in the truck, and the driver asked for my address.

Crap. I didn't know.

I told him, "Bunsuri." He asked which number, since there are a lot of neighborhood areas named *Bunsuri*. So, I told him we had this one commemorative statue like the one down the road.

He said, "Every neighborhood out here has them. Any other things you can remember?"

I said, "There is a super nice house nearby, and it looks very American."

He laughed and said, "Oh, I know what you're talking about." After about thirty minutes of driving around, we found the shipping container.

Even though they had proven to be somewhat trustworthy by not kidnapping me, I still had my guard up and didn't want them to know precisely where I lived. I told them to drop me off on the corner, thanked them for the ride, and waited until they drove off. Then I headed toward the container.

When I walked up, I saw a lot of shoes outside, which meant my mother was inside teaching. I decided to sit outside and wait until her class was done. When the doors opened, my mother saw me and was shocked.

"Where have you been? Why didn't you call me? Oh my God, oh my God, I forgot! How did you get here? Did you walk?"

I told her she was supposed to pick me up from the bus stop near the military base. She hadn't shown up, so I'd walked home.

I was still wearing my damp gym class uniform, and when I got inside, I felt super hot, and my shin was itchy. I rolled up my pant leg and noticed my ankle was brown. I thought it was strange. I continued rolling up my pant leg and realized my ankle wasn't brown from dirt; it was brown from dried-up blood. I pulled up my pant leg further.

I looked down and said, "Mom, look!"

My mother screamed! There was dried blood everywhere and a twenty-centimeter diagonal gash across my shin. She started crying, then ran to get some peroxide and ointment. When she began to clean away the dried blood, you could finally see how deep it was. The white meat was exposed or possibly my bone. It was bad. She cleaned it up and put Band-Aids up and down my leg, hoping to hold together the wound.

After a week, I finally went to the dermatologist to get it looked at. He chastised me, asking why I had waited so long to see him. "Since you didn't come in sooner, now you will have a scar, which is very unbecoming for a woman."

I didn't appreciate the male chauvinism. I wasn't even in pain; I only wanted to get it checked out because it wasn't healing properly. I just was so used to acting like nothing ever happened and truthfully afraid to feel it. I didn't want to cause any other issues at home and be a bigger burden than I already was.

Koreans spend most of their time outside of school studying. I wasn't like other Korean students. They were more concerned about testing, and I was concerned about getting the fuck out of the house. Plus, we were always having tests. We'd have standardized testing four weeks out of the year.

I hated those weeks because I hated tests. I was only interested in things like history, art, and gym class. Science, math, language arts, and technology were not my strong suits, and those subjects comprised the bulk of our standardized testing.

I also loved those weeks, because it meant we got out of school early—I got to be free and hang out with my friends, which meant I wasn't at home with my father. We'd run around, having fun until they had to go to *hagwon* or home for lunch. The first couple of hours were a lot of fun until they left, and I had to spend the rest of the day wandering around the city, trying to find something to keep me occupied and out of trouble from the afternoon until late at night—sometimes twelve hours just waiting alone—until my mother picked me up after work to go to the shipping container.

Some days, I would try to go to two of my close friends' places when they were called home for lunch—partly hoping to get a bite to eat (though I usually just had to watch them eat), but mostly because I didn't want to be stuck outside alone with nothing to do.

One day, we were walking together after school, and they gave each other a look, then suddenly started running. I was athletic and strong, so I caught them—by the backs of their necks—thinking it was a game. Then one of them finally blurted out, "We don't like that you try to come over all the time. You're not invited. Why do you always follow us home? Go to your own house. My mom doesn't even like me hanging out with you anyway."

That hurt like hell. My pride just crashed to the ground. I had a knot in my throat from trying not to cry. After that, I mostly stayed outside alone—hungry, cold, or hot, I can't even remember the weather anymore—just outside for hours every single day.

And all of it was getting to me. Why did everybody reject me? My friends. Their parents. My own mother. My sister basically had my mom—she was the sunshine of her life, best friends with her. But what about me?

In the mornings, my father drove us all into the city. He insisted on always driving with the windows down, even in the dead middle of winter. Did he give a fuck that I was sitting in the backseat, windows open, cold air blasting me, shivering as my wet hair started to form icicles? Nope. Not at all. He said we needed "fresh air."

In fact, the day after my friends told me their mothers didn't want me around, my father was driving us into the city. We were coming up to the top of the mountain when, out of nowhere, he asked me, "Where were you yesterday after your testing?"

"Hanging out with my friends," I said hesitantly, without really thinking about the consequences. I mean, it was the truth. That's what everyone did on the last day of testing. No one studies—we just hang out. I didn't think anything of it until—

Oh shit. That wasn't the right answer.

He started cursing and yelling at me. "You're a stupid fucking bitch!" He went off about how I should've been studying and kept screaming, "Why the hell were you with your friends?"

Maybe it was the fresh emotional wound from my friends' rejection, or maybe it was this gnawing feeling like I was completely alone in the world, all swirling in the back of my mind, but I exploded like a volcano. This time, I had had it.

I fired back, "Where was I supposed to go? Why couldn't I have fun with my friends? It was the last day of the test. What did you expect me to do while I waited for hours?"

As soon as those words left my mouth, he pulled the car over and jumped out. My sister's eyes popped out of her head, her jaw dropped, and she was just gleeful—not giggling exactly, more like smirking—excited to see what was about to happen to me.

My father was standing outside my door, violently screaming, "Get the fuck out of the car!" I was pissed by this point. Why the fuck did I need to get out?

My dad yanked me out of the car at the top of that freezing mountain. He started smacking the shit out of me, calling me a stupid bitch at the top of his lungs. Just hitting me. Repeatedly.

My head throbbed. I didn't know what the fuck was going on. My mother jumped out too—not because she had the guts to stand up to him (she never did), but screaming purely out of fear. He ended up hitting her too, hard enough to chip her tooth.

I got back in the car and—*fuck*!—my nose was bleeding. I grabbed a tissue and pinched my nose to stop the bleeding—and *fuck*!—there were blood splashes on my white school uniform shirt. I kept pinching my nose the entire ride down the mountain and into the city, with the windows still rolled down, of course. My sister was snickering. She laughed at me for getting my ass beat. She did that shit all the time.

I eventually got to school with specks of blood on my shirt, which either no one noticed or they did and didn't say anything. Regardless, the constant throbbing in my head was a steady reminder all day of what had happened.

I waited until the blood had clotted in my nose, then blew it to get the rest out. I had become an expert at stopping a nosebleed.

It was at this point I finally realized—not only is all this not normal, it is completely fucked up. My heart was so heavy. This weight inside my chest pulled me down, made it hard to breathe. And the throbbing just beat it further into my brain: *I am not loved.*

Still, I didn't want anyone to ask questions. I felt it was my duty to protect my family, no matter what was happening behind closed doors. I didn't want the world to know. That silence felt like loyalty. And I was very loyal and protective of my family. I had my own issues with them, but that didn't stop me from defending them. This sentiment definitely extended to my best friends as well because they were like family in my eyes. If someone fucked with them, it was over. I didn't play around.

As part of our school curriculum, we were required to do community service work. Jieun and I ended up doing our service hours at the post office. We rolled up to do some work and Jieun pulled me aside. She was angered by a group of girls hanging out by the post office, pointing at the biggest one and saying that this girl had picked on her. Now, I was tiny back then and very short for my age, but I was thick and tough. Jieun was about one-third my size. To a group of older girls—big, tall, rough ones—we looked like frail little things that they could push around. They were known as the bad girls from the bad high school.

Jieun and I went inside, sat down on the couch in the lobby, and were just talking to each other when the group of girls approached us. The biggest, tallest, and roughest-looking one walked over, staring down at us as if that were intimidating. She didn't know who she was dealing with.

"What are you looking at?" she snarled at us with this menace in her eyes. I laughed as I normally do when shit is about to go down. I don't know if it's the adrenaline or what, but I can feel my body is ready for whatever happens next.

She glared at Jieun. "You wanna get beat up?" Jieun stood up, and the girl slapped her.

But before that hand made it completely across Jieun's face, I was midair, leaping off the couch and onto this beastly girl. I knocked her to the ground, and I don't know what happened next because I blacked out. When I came to, I had three grown-ass men ripping me off her. There was hair everywhere and some blood on the ground and on our clothes—not mine, hers. She was still lying on the floor, curled up, trying to protect herself as if I were still attacking her. She finally stood up—weak and shaky like a newborn calf, in complete shock, and disoriented, looking like she had no idea where she was. Probably the first time she'd ever been beaten up. And it was by little ole me.

When rage came over me, I lost it. I completely lost it. I wailed on her, beating her senseless. I didn't even think; I just jumped. I did what I had to do to protect my best friend, who was like my family. Although I hate admitting it, it was also a great way to channel all my anger and just let it out.

For a moment, I was worried. What if my parents found out? I didn't want her to go to the cops. But then I realized that would mean she'd have to admit she got her ass beat by me, which would embarrass the hell out of her. Chances were, I was safe. While this scared me—knowing that I had this anger within me—I knew it was also my power. This rage could protect those I loved most, but it was also a reminder that not only do I look like my father, I have his temperament within me as well. That was a hard pill to swallow.

After the incident, Jieun and I were berated and kicked out. We didn't care; we felt on top of the world. We also got in trouble later and lost all our community hours, but it was worth it. No one could fuck with us.

Back at home, my mother applied for a $10,000 single-mother business loan, so she could open up her own studio again. These loans were designed for divorced or single mothers to start their business at low interest rates. The catch is you have to be single in order to get it. I'm not entirely sure when or how it happened, but some years back, my mother had convinced my father to get a divorce. For years she pleaded with him to allow her to get a divorce simply so she could qualify for these loans to help the family out. She would approach him when he was in a good mood and try to sweet-talk him into signing the papers. After years of placating him and appeasing his ego, she ended up getting him to sign. I don't know exactly how she convinced him, but she did.

But they were only legally divorced on paper; my mom stayed with him. She had told my father it was only so she could take advantage of assistance for single mothers. Eventually she would get away, but for now, she knew she was stuck. No matter where she went, he would find her.

Once she got the loan, she bought this really awesome space closer to our school. It was a storefront business with metal gates that came down at night to cover the windows facing the street. Inside was one giant room with all of the art supplies and desks and a second, smaller room separated from the main space with a glass window. There we had a small office with a desk, a kitchenette, and an area in the corner that had a drain where my mom hooked up a shower nozzle, so we could clean ourselves. There was also a sliding partition that could close off the other half of the smaller room where we had a computer, TV, and area for kids to play. But no toilet. That was in the building hallway under the stairs, just like our first studio in Seoul. You know how much I hate using hallway bathrooms under the stairs. I'm not saying because I dreaded going up the hallway under the stairs in the middle of the night that I would pee in the makeshift shower. But I'm also not saying that I didn't. You can draw your own conclusions.

I ended up spending most of my time sleeping there, under the desk, and my sister would sleep on the floor near the TV and computer. My parents would toggle between the shipping container and the art studio. This is where we would spend the next year of my life.

CHAPTER 5

A Wounded Animal Is a Dangerous One

I typically stayed in the art studio throughout most of high school, by myself, instead of constantly traveling back and forth to the shipping container. It was close to my school, only a short bus ride away. Plus, a good portion of the time, my father stayed in the shipping container, so our interactions were kept at a minimum. At this point, I had come to the full realization that my father was somebody I didn't want to be in the same room with.

Except for one time, toward the end of my first year of high school, I came home to our new art studio to study and waited for my mom to come home. I walked in, and to my surprise, there he was—my father, by himself.

Shit. Just him and me.

I nodded in acknowledgment as I walked past him in the main room and continued on my way. I figured I would pretend to study in the office behind the room divider—anything to avoid him. I sat down at the desk, which wasn't just a desk. Underneath it was my "room." That tiny space under the desk was where I slept, where I spent my time—the only shred of privacy I had as a teenage girl. It was important to me in a way I couldn't even explain.

I had just settled there when my father called to me from the other side of the divider.

Shit. What does he want now?

"What have you been up to these days in school?"

I blanked on an answer.

He said, "Bring me all your textbooks."

I grabbed one and walked into the other room to present it to him.

"I said, 'bring me all your textbooks.'"

I returned to my desk, grabbed the rest of the books, and knelt down in front of him to present them. He grabbed one from the stack and flipped through it, asking, "Where are you in this book?"

I sensed he was getting angry, but I had no clue why. I looked up at him and pointed to where we were in the book.

"So, you're learning? Because I don't see any notes," he yelled at me.

I opened my mouth to say something.

Whack! He struck me on the head with the book. Over and over again.

Each hit felt like it split my skull open. A sharp, ringing shock exploded in my brain every time the book landed. My eyes watered uncontrollably—not just from fear but from the sheer jarring impact. I could feel my scalp starting to swell, little hot lumps already forming under the skin.

What the fuck is going on?

Harder and harder, he kept whaling on me with the book. Tearing the pages. Ripping apart my books. Hitting me harder on the head.

When the book wasn't enough, he started punching my head with his fist. My ears buzzed so loudly, the sound of his fists connecting with my skull felt distant—like it was happening underwater. My jaw rattled with every punch. My teeth slammed together so hard I was terrified they would crack.

I cried and screamed my lungs out in pain and anger for him to stop.

He hit more. He hit harder.

I tried to block my head and shield my body from the blows. I stood my ground. I wasn't about to apologize like my mom or sister—I hadn't done anything to deserve this. My pride wouldn't let me curl up and just get beaten up without trying to defend myself.

Then he began to kick me all over, and I finally gave in. I curled up into a ball on the floor to protect myself.

He kicked my body again and again. More pain. More screams. Repeatedly punching and kicking me.

The kicks landed on my ribs, my back, my stomach—each one a bolt of agony that stole my breath. I tried to squeeze myself smaller, to make myself less of a target, but it didn't matter. The pain radiated through me like hot knives.

It wasn't just the pain. It was the humiliation.

I was nothing to him. Just something to destroy.

I was a girl—fragile and small—trying to hold my own organs together under the force of his feet. My mind couldn't keep up. There was just pain. Pain. Pain.

Exhausted, he stopped.

He shouted at me to get back on my knees. As I started crying my lungs out, he punched me on the side of my head and yelled, "Keep crying if you want to die."

I stopped crying.

He said, "Get the fuck out of my face."

I gathered myself together, stood up, walked back to my desk, and sat down. I quietly sobbed to myself, trying not to make any noise—because I wasn't allowed to show any emotions in front of him. I tasted iron in my mouth. My ears rang so intensely that the silence felt louder than any scream.

I tried to suck the tears back into my eyes. To erase them. To be invisible.

My body shook on its own. I hugged my sides like that might hold me together—like I might spill out of myself.

But did you think he was done?

Oh, no.

That motherfucker came storming up to my desk with a large glass bottle, lunging at me, about to smash it over my head, and shouting at the top of his lungs, "Shut the fuck up! Stop fucking crying before I kill you!"

I immediately stopped crying and stared right into his eyes in complete defiance.

Holding the bottle over his head, he froze and glared at me in pure rage. Pissed off, he left the office and sat in the other room for a bit before leaving the studio.

At last—relief.

I sat in the silence for a moment, bewildered at what had just occurred. I felt the pain all over my body and heard a ringing in my ears—that pulsating high-pitched noise. I looked down at my olive-green pants and noticed blood on my crotch.

Shock washed over me.

What the fuck just happened?

I pulled down my pants and, to my horror, blood was leaking out of my vagina.

My heart dropped into a dark pit in my stomach.

For a split second, I wondered if I had somehow lost my virginity from being beaten.

The blood felt wrong. Dirty. Like it was proof of something ruined inside of me.

Am I broken now?

I felt a hot, crawling shame between my legs. He had kicked me so hard and so many times while I was on the ground that he had fucking made my vagina bleed. My head pounded from being continuously beaten with a book and his fists. My entire body ached.

It wasn't just physical pain. I felt contaminated.

I didn't want to touch myself there. Didn't want to clean it. I hated that the blood was coming from inside me—that it was proof of how deeply he had hurt me.

I felt guilty, like somehow it was my fault my body had responded this way. Maybe if I had been stronger, if I hadn't cried, he wouldn't have kicked me so many times. Maybe my body wouldn't have been betraying me now.

I took off my pants and tried my best to clean the blood, scrubbing at the stain. No use. It was in there.

I grabbed a pad and put it in my underwear to absorb the blood coming from between my legs.

I was only fifteen.

I slept in the studio alone that night, under my desk—my "room." I felt safe under there. It was my own private space. I felt like no one could see me in my little "room."

As I lay there, thoughts ran through my head. A lot of thoughts.

It was the first time I really recognized how fucked up all this was. This wasn't normal. My father wasn't normal. I just couldn't wrap my head around not only what had happened that night, but all my life. It was like my whole childhood had cracked wide open in that moment.

The ringing in my ears felt almost gentle now, like a lullaby. I let it carry me away, because thinking hurt too much. Because if I really thought about it, I might have started crying again.

And he had told me exactly what would happen if I did.

The ringing in my ears continued, but the sound was almost soothing.

The next day, my mother came to the studio. She asked me what I ate, and we made small talk. All the while, I played it off as if nothing had happened with my father last night. She kept telling me to look up at her because I kept looking down, unable to make eye contact. After a few minutes of holding back the anger, finally I just said, *Fuck it,* and told her the truth. She screamed, enraged at my father, yelling at the top of her lungs in anger at him—sobbing over what he had done to me.

She held me for a moment, trembling with rage, grief, guilt—maybe all of it. But as quickly as her anger toward him surfaced, it disappeared back into the silence we always returned to. Nothing else was said. We just sat there, side by side, in the tension of unspoken truths. That was the thing about our family—we could erupt, cry, scream, but somehow still find ourselves right back in the quiet. The kind that doesn't heal. The kind that keeps everything buried.

My mom and my sister were like best friends, but as much as I admired their connection, I couldn't help but feel so alone. They had each other. I didn't have anyone. I idealized the kind of mother-daughter relationship where the daughter confides in her mother about everything, and they talk about their dreams and aspirations. But I had been keeping everything to myself for so long—pretending I was fine through it all, just so I wouldn't add to my mother's worries—that I didn't even know how to be that kind of daughter to her. The sad part is, I became that way to protect her, and she ended up making fun of me for it. I had become so distant, and I rarely spoke. She used to say my insides were dark just like the famous Korean black noodle dish *jajangmyeon.* I was an emotionally torn teenager; angst was my normal state.

Although my sister had already started college, she was still living at home, and spending all her free time studying like a good Korean student. My mother had sent her to *hagwon,* the private academies, to study after school in high school to prepare her for college. And even throughout college, she was sent to *hagwons* for private instruction.

Did I get to go to *hagwon* to help me with my studies like my sister and all my friends? Nope. But that was my sister, and she got what she wanted. My mother always defended her too because my sister could never be wrong. She was her dream child, or at least my mom wanted her to be. My mom had such high hopes for my sister, and she acted the part. She was studying all the time, and she was really athletic. So perfect for the dream my mother had for a perfect daughter.

I had come home from school to the art studio when my sister was already in there, reading and studying as usual. We typically argued and fought, but on this particular day things escalated. My sister began by just starting a petty argument—and back and forth, we were bickering with each other. Then all of a sudden, she uppercut me in the back of my head. *Whack*! I was in a daze, trying to regain my consciousness while my brain was strategizing how I was going to fuck her up.

Once I get my power back, you're dead, bitch!

I was about to lose it. My full consciousness was back, and I was in attack mode. My sister had beaten me up all my life, and I let her—I don't know why. Perhaps because my mom always gave me this feeling that my sister was untouchable. She got a pass on everything. She was the golden child, and I was just there.

Finally, I said, *Fuck it*!

I fought back, wrestling her on the floor, hitting, scratching, kicking, and biting. Now, my sister is stronger than me, and four and a half years older, but I didn't care. I was like a feral animal going wild on her. Eventually, both of us exhausted, we stopped.

She left the studio pissed off at me. And while I didn't necessarily win this fight, I had fought back, and that was good enough for me.

My mother came to the studio and told me that I would be staying at the shipping container that weekend. So much for having an entire weekend away from my father. When I got inside the container, my sister and my mother were there. Folded arms, my mother instructed me to "sit on the floor."

My mother grabbed my sister by the arm, pulled up the sleeve of her light blue Ralph Lauren shirt, which was a reminder that I did not own any name-brand clothes, and pointed to her arm.

"Look at your sister's arm!"

Yes, those were my bite marks on her arm. *Whack*! My mother hit me. My sister was behind her giving me a smirk because I was getting in trouble for a fight she started.

"What if she can't get married now because of this? What if it scars?" *Whack*! She hit me again.

But don't worry about my scars, right? Or her hitting me? Or finding out the truth about who started it? Because none of that mattered. I had no one on my side. My father abused me. My sister beat me up. And now my mom did, too.

She didn't even ask me what happened. She just took what my sister had said, and that was it. She always did that. And now more than ever, it felt like me against the world. Plus, I think my sister kind of knew that I wasn't going to say shit and took total advantage of it.

Before the end of my first year of high school, my mother had put out ads to increase the number of students she taught. Not because she wanted more money or even necessarily more students, but so she could pack in the place to look more appealing for someone to purchase the studio from her. And it worked. She ended up selling the place for $10,000 more than it was worth, paid off the loan she had taken out on the studio, pocketed the extra money, and started teaching once a week at the shipping container instead.

It just so happened that the old woman who owned the art studio building and lived alone on the top floor had a room she wanted to rent out to a student. My mother thought it would be convenient for me to stay in this room above her former studio, so I didn't have to commute for school, and I could stay through the winter break.

It wasn't the best space, but I liked it because I didn't have to put up with my sister, nor did I have to see my dad. To me, that was amazing enough. It was a pretty empty room except for a desk and a computer. It had heated floors but no heater in the room, which is typical of Korean homes. It was already dipping below freezing outside, so the minimal heat emitting from the floor was barely enough to keep the house warm.

However, this old lady knew my financial situation, and she definitely treated me like it. That heated floor in my room? It got turned off. The hot water for my shower? Turned off, too. Why did she do this? I concluded she did this for two reasons: the first being she didn't want to spend money on me to keep me warm even though my mother had paid her rent; the second being she was a crusty old bitch who wanted to make me suffer because she was heartless.

Every morning, I'd take freezing-cold showers—but not all at once. I couldn't. It was too cold for that. I'd start by washing my lower body first, still wearing my top, then quickly switch—take my top off, wash my upper body, dry off, get dressed, and only then wash my hair, still fully clothed. I washed my hair every single morning before school, just like I still do now.

There was no bathtub—just a sink, a little Korean bathroom chair, and a drain in the floor. I remember staring down into that drain every day while I washed my hair, somehow getting lost in it. It almost gave me this strange illusion I couldn't explain—something I'd always remember. My head would get so cold while I scrubbed that I'd actually get brain freezes.

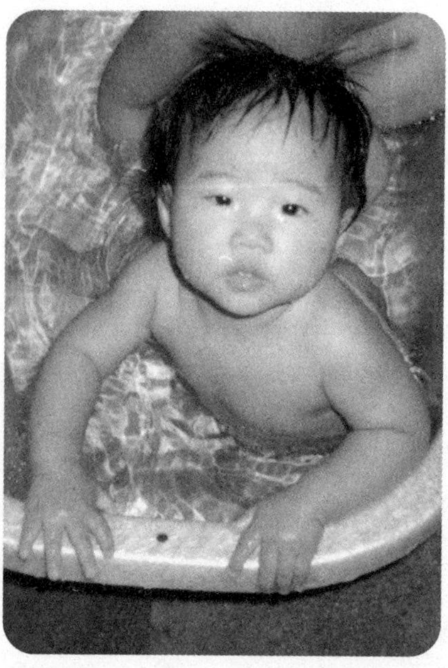

My sister and I used to "shower" in this tiny bathroom with no tub, just a basin on the ground and a shower hose attached to the wall. Taken in 1985 in Seoul, South Korea. Courtesy of Jungok Kim.

But I made sure I kept myself clean and bathed no matter what. Nobody was going to make fun of me for smelling bad or looking dirty. I already didn't have the things other kids had—at least they couldn't take that dignity from me.

Every night it would drop below freezing with no heat coming up from the floor. I would layer on my clothes, as many as I possibly could. Ten pairs of pants, three jackets, hats, scarves, whatever I had in the room. If Mari was with me, we would huddle together for warmth. I couldn't really keep Mari there with me all the time because the old lady didn't like it. It got harder and harder every day to live in those conditions. Going through this for just one day is hard but staying constantly cold in the room while I was awake, taking cold showers, and going to sleep every day was pushing me to my limits. In the middle of the night, I woke up to see the old lady standing over me and staring. She had this look in her eye like, "Why the fuck does she have all those clothes on?" I always slept right by the door, because the door was warmed by the heat she had for herself in the living room. So, when she opened the door, she woke me up—but I acted as if I was sleeping to see what she would do. She just stared me down for a little bit and left.

She made me feel less than. She treated me like I had no worth and made me feel like shit. This is why we never told anyone we were poor: they treat you like this. I started seeing for myself why my mom told me to keep that secret and never ever tell anyone.

My mother would come by to check in on me and ask how everything was. I'd tell her it was a little cold, but that it was okay. The old lady insisted, "Oh no, the heat is on." My mother never questioned her, and I didn't go against her word because I just knew the problem wasn't going to be fixed. On one hand, I'm treated like shit by this old lady, and I'm freezing to death—but on the other hand, I'm not at home with my father. And the last thing I wanted was to be near my father.

One day, she left the house for a few hours, leaving me home alone. My mission was to find the switches for the floor and water heaters—and I did. I cranked that shit up all the way. For the first time since I had lived there, I had a hot shower and a heated floor. It felt so great. I closed my eyes, lying on that hot-ass heated floor, and it reminded me of being underneath my mom's blanket in my old apartment in Gyeonggi-do. In the wintertime, my mom always had a blanket on the floor in her room, and the heated floor would get really hot underneath the blanket. I would always run to my mom's blanket when I got home after school and just hide my whole body underneath. It was so warm, and it smelled like my mom. Just thinking about that time made me smile.

Until, that is, the crusty old bitch came home and turned the heat off. When she was gone again, I'd turn it all back on. And she'd turn them off. Then I'd turn them back on. This battle only went on briefly because I didn't want to get kicked out.

The year was ending, and the holidays were approaching. Although we were Christians, our family didn't really celebrate the holidays.

But this old bitch did, and her entire family had come over for Christmas to celebrate together. I decided not to leave the room under any circumstances. I was too embarrassed, and I just didn't want any more people in this world to know about my situation. I stayed in my room locked away in the cold, playing on my computer all day, chatting with friends through messenger or email. I didn't even leave the room to go pee. Not that I needed to because I didn't eat or drink all day anyway.

All the while, I could hear them in the other room right outside my door having a great time, playing games, laughing, and joking. I could hear her speaking to her family in the kindest, most loving tone. This solemnity washed over me as I realized, *This is how normal people live.*

Who the fuck was this lady? And what did she do with that crusty old bitch? The scents of food flooded my nose all day as I tried to ignore the rumbling in my stomach from not eating. It was pure torture. I thought about how she treated her family and everyone else with dignity because she saw them as people. To her, I was poor—nothing but an animal. And that's how she treated me. Like an animal.

All of a sudden, the door to my room opened. I startled, thinking it was the old lady coming in for something. I looked up, and it was one of her grandchildren, staring at me like I was some homeless girl squatting in their grandmother's house.

"Grandma, who is this?"

"She's nobody."

Nobody? Are you serious?

I listened to them all night enjoying themselves while I sat at my desk still chatting with my friends and acting like I was spending this holiday just as happy as they were. After everyone had left to go to karaoke, the old lady entered my room with a plate of food. She handed it to me with a huge smile on her face after having such a great time with her family. I think she forgot who I was or something because she never smiled at me. I took the plate and said thank you, and she left. I was so hungry that the moment the door closed, I started shoving the food in my mouth.

As I slowed down, I noticed little things about the plate she had fixed for me. Upon further inspection, I realized that it wasn't a plate made for me—it was a collection of scraps. A tear started to form in my eyes. I grappled with the reality I was literally being treated like an animal. That feeling of worthlessness just sank into the pit of my stomach. I tried to force down my last bite, swallowing down the food along with my pride as the tears came streaming down my face.

Instead of letting this tear me down, it made me realize that I need to do better than this. I need to do better than my parents. I need to make money, so no one ever treats me like a fucking animal ever again. I will hustle and bust my ass. And when I finally get rich, I will never treat anyone the way people have treated me. I will always treat people the same, no matter how much money they have, their job, or their position in life. I couldn't wait to finish school, so I could be grown up and just leave this place. Leave this country and just move to America, where I'd be free to do whatever I want.

Before the start of my second year of high school, I left the apartment with the old lady. My mother could no longer afford it. She had taken out another loan for "single mothers" to get another new studio about a fifteen-to-twenty-minute walk to my high school. We moved out of the shipping container for reasons I don't fully understand, but there we were—together again, as a family under one roof.

Fuck.

On the outside, the new studio looked similar to our previous one, storefront windows with a roll-up gate. But inside was not the same at all. In the front was the entire studio for my mother's art students. Behind the main room was a door that led to a toilet. On one side of the toilet was a door to a small room that became my sister's own private room. To the left was the rest of the living area, which consisted of a small kitchenette, small table, couch, back door, and an area in the kitchen that had a drain on the floor with a showerhead attached to the bottom of the wall. This is where we showered. In the middle of the kitchen.

When I questioned why my sister got her own room, my mom said she "needs her own space, so she can study because she is in college." But in Korea, high school students are typically treated better than anyone else because of the importance of getting good enough grades to make it into a reputable university. Once you're in university, you are still treated with that respect—but the pressure they put on high school students to succeed is ridiculous. Parents spend so much money on tutors and *hagwons,* but not for me. Even in college, my mom was still paying for my sister to go to a *hagwon*—but again, not me. Like, weren't we poor? How did my family afford this? Somehow, my mom would make it happen by borrowing money or writing a heartfelt letter to whoever was in charge.

I slept on the ground between the clothing rack next to the couch and the kitchen table. It was like my own little area. My parents would sleep in the studio when all the students had left. When I came home after school, I had to be extra quiet so as not to attract attention from the students. They weren't to know I was there and that we lived behind the bathroom door. I wasn't even allowed to turn on any lights.

In the beginning of living in the new studio, my father wasn't around much. He was doing "things," as he said, and I have no clue what that meant. He could have been working odd jobs or scheming up one of his latest ideas. One time, he was gone for an entire month. Like, just gone. And no one questioned where he was. I was excited at the prospect of him not coming back.

That was a good month, but sadly it ended, and he eventually came back.

Along with the pressure of making sure no one knew I was poor and keeping up with my studies, I was also faced with the increasing prevalence of materialism in high school. My friends all had designer and name-brand bags, shoes, clothes, cell phones with selfie cameras, touch screens, everything. I had my two-dollar slide shoes that everyone knew were worth only two dollars. I was ridiculed for not having name-brand things. I did my best to hide my shame and my lack of money, but I couldn't keep up anymore. And when my friends questioned why I had second-hand clothes, mostly my mother's clothes that she used to wear when she was younger, I would play it off. I would say I was cool with it, that vintage was my style. I certainly wasn't about to admit that I couldn't afford anything else.

But guess who did get nice new clothes all the time? My sister, of course. How she afforded it, I never knew. When I'd ask to borrow her clothes, she would always refuse—and my mother wasn't going to force her to let me borrow them either.

I had pressure from school with my studies, my living situation, my fucked-up family, my materialistic friends, and let's not forget about the teachers who still beat the shit out of me because they could get away with it. Just all this pressure from everywhere, and I felt like a powder keg about to explode.

I carried on like this for months and got nowhere with my mother. She had repeatedly made me promises over the years to start buying me my own things once my sister went to college, but she failed to keep those promises. You want to know who finally asked me, "What's wrong?" To my surprise—and I would suspect yours as well—it was my dad! I was shocked.

So, I told him I needed money, so I could buy things. I didn't have good shoes, a coat, a backpack, socks, or anything nice for school. He listened and handed me $700 to go shopping and buy myself something new.

What in the actual fuck?

Did my dad just do something nice for me?

Also, where did he get $700?!?

Even recalling this more than twenty years later, it still shocks me that this happened. My dad of all people. So crazy.

It was my first time ever going shopping to buy something new with my own money to spend. I bought a bunch of new clothes, specifically Calvin Klein jeans, white Air Force 1 high-tops, and my Nike slides for school. No more two-dollar slides. They were name-brand, and I loved them.

After I bought my new clothes, I noticed one day that my Calvins were missing. I looked everywhere for them. In walked my sister wearing my fucking Calvins. I was pissed. I was just about to speak when my mother told me to shut up. I started going off on her, and she said, "What's the big deal? She had to go to her class. Leave her alone." I stopped and looked at her like *what the fuck.* She said, "Your sister is in college. She needs to look good." Again, fuck me, right?

The one thing that kept me somewhat sane throughout high school was Yoon-gi. It's hard to explain how it all evolved, where it started, and why he was important. I mean, when we first met in the beginning of high school, he used to tease me and laugh at my thickness. Like, is this really how boys flirt? He wasn't the only one. My family, teachers, and society all judged me for having thick thighs. They never bothered me; I never gave a fuck. But I gave a fuck about Yoon-gi.

Yoon-gi was popular. He was a top student, played sports, tall, super good-looking, and everyone wanted him. For some reason though he paid attention to me. He would never admit that he liked me, at least not for a couple years.

As Yoon-gi and I became closer, the more he became inquisitive about my family life and where I lived. As you know, I was not about to tell anyone the truth, much less him. At this point, I didn't even know what we were other than two people hanging out all the time and coyly flirting with one another. It was innocent. But that's not what everyone else thought. They would always ask us if we were together, and we'd always deny it. Our relationship started off with insults, which eventually led to mild flirtation, and then we were hanging out all the time. So much so that Jieun felt like she was being pushed aside as my best friend over spending time with Yoon-gi. Essentially, she felt like I was breaking up with her to be with him. My teachers even figured it out and pulled me aside to tell me that he deserved someone so much better. That I needed to leave him alone because I was a bad influence on him. Shit, that was his choice. He was the one who wanted to hang with me; I wasn't pushing the matter.

His family owned a house, which is a big deal in Korea. Most people live in apartments or condos, but his family had enough money to own an actual, stand-alone house. He came from a good family, studied hard, and was kind to everyone. Even me. When the insults abated, and the flirtation started, I actually began to feel good about myself. After going over to his house several times over the years, he insisted that he finally see where I live.

Fuck! I can't show him that!

I didn't know how to tell him the truth, so I didn't. I told him it was too far, too inconvenient, and suggested we go to my mother's art studio instead. It was close by, and it looked presentable enough. What he didn't know was that I wasn't just visiting—I lived there. I walked him through the space like it was just a casual after-school hangout spot. I pointed out brushes, canvases, shelves like I was giving a tour, pretending I'd go home later when really…I wouldn't.

What made Yoon-gi different was that he actually saw me. He didn't just help me study—he helped me care. Helped me try. The things I didn't give a shit about before? I started showing up for them just because he believed I could. He made me feel like I mattered.

The shift from "just friends" to something more wasn't dramatic. There wasn't some grand confession. It was slow, soft. A brush of a cheek, a longer look, studying together at the studio turning into stolen kisses in the back when we knew no one was around. It wasn't official, but it was real.

By my final year of high school, everyone knew we were together. My teachers still hated me, my father was still an asshole, but in the last six months of the year, I finally had gotten my own room. My mother decided it was time I had my own space, and without any opposition, my sister agreed. She didn't care; she wasn't living there anymore anyhow. I was ecstatic.

One day after school, I decided to take a short nap on the floor between the couch and the clothing rack. In the front part of the studio, my mother was teaching her class, so I had to be super quiet. I was dead asleep when I felt something brush up against me. I opened one eye to see what it was, and right there in front of my face was a big-ass rat the size of my forearm. Its tail was just as long as its body.

I wanted to scream. But I couldn't, because I wasn't allowed to make any noises after school. My mom's students weren't supposed to know I was there. I was mortified, but the rat just walked on by me unbothered and scurried out through a small crack by the back door. Bugs, mice, rats—I had encountered all of them living in that studio. I needed to get the fuck out of there.

For college, I made the decision that I wanted to go to either Hongik, my first choice—which is where you want to go if you're pursuing a good art career—or Chugye University, which was my second choice. My grades were shit except for the subjects I loved, which included art of course. But excelling in one subject wasn't good enough to get into university. In Korea, if you don't get into college, people look down on you. You will have a hard time getting a job; you're basically shunned from society. So Yoon-gi helped me study, and surer than shit, my final year of school I did a decent job with my grades. Normally my grades were pretty shit, but they jumped up to high grades because of his help.

My mother surprised me in the final half of my last year of high school by sending me to a *hagwon*. We couldn't afford it, so she wrote a letter to an old college friend who ran a college-prep art *hagwon* asking them if they would allow me to attend classes for free as a favor to her. Her friend obliged.

The *hagwon* was in Seoul, about a forty-five-minute bus ride from Gyeonggi-do. I would take the bus after school to Seoul, oftentimes sitting with Yoon-gi in tow and making out along the way. The *hagwon* was full of pretentious rich kids, and I didn't feel like I fit in. I was also embarrassed because the teachers all knew I was going there for free because I was too poor to pay. They didn't care whether or not I showed up. Pretty much every day after school we'd go to Seoul for my *hagwon* studies from about 5:00 p.m. until 10:00 p.m. Did I go? Yes. But did I go the entire time? Hell no.

We'd get to Seoul around 5:00 p.m. and just fuck around until 9:00 or 9:30, killing time until the final half hour of *hagwon* class just to show face. I learned more from teaching myself art than I did at the *hagwon.* Don't get me wrong: I wasn't ungrateful that I finally had gotten into a *hagwon* just like my friends and my sister. I just no longer cared—I really only cared about being with Yoon-gi. I did show up, so they wouldn't tell my mother I never came. I owed her that much.

I painted these two pieces at my in-person entrance exam for Chugye University—still life is uninspiring but man I can paint. Created in 2003 in Seoul, South Korea. Artist: Young Bae

I ended up applying to both my top colleges of choice: Chugye and Hongik Universities. Aside from the standardized university entrance exam, sort of like the SAT or ACT in the United States, and my high school grades, these art schools required you to sit for an in-person art exam. These exams typically lasted five hours. They'd sit you down in a studio amongst the other students applying to art school and reveal a piece of art that you had to either paint or draw, depending on the medium they chose.

I went to my art exam at Hongik University, which is known as the best art college in Korea. I was sitting in the exam studio, and in the center of the room was a sheet covering some kind of art we'd have to replicate. Our medium was watercolors, and let me tell you, while I do like watercolors, I don't like painting statues with them. They pulled off the sheet, and it was a fucking statue. It just wasn't for me—and I felt like a robot doing it.

I didn't get into Hongik University, but I wasn't mad about it. My art exam for Chugye was completely different. When I showed up, they allowed us to use any type of medium we wanted. The most important thing to them was to have fun with what we were doing, and that's exactly what I did. I used watercolors, pastels, colored pencils—you name it!

I ended up getting into Chugye University to study printmaking. It wasn't even the fact that I got into a great art school that had me excited; it was because I was just that much closer to freedom. I knew my time in Korea was growing shorter, and I could feel it. I could taste it.

The prospect of going to a new school also meant I would meet new friends. New friends who didn't know me. New friends who didn't know my old lies. Now I had a chance to leave all that behind. I could just move forward. I could live a seemingly "normal" life.

CHAPTER 6

THE ESCAPE PLAN

If you haven't seen the 2020 Academy Award Best Picture *Parasite,* you should. Not only because it's a masterpiece by Korean director Bong Joon Ho (shout-out to Korea for winning Best Picture, Best Director, Best Original Screenplay, and Best International Feature Film), but it's a great way to see how Koreans treat each other based on socio-economic status. You can see how we live, how we dress, where we go. To me, the Kim family in the film is like the Bae side of my family. And the Park family is like my mom's side.

Just as I was settling into the idea of "this is as bad as it gets" at home, my mother's art studio stopped pulling in students. She wasn't making as much money due to some new government-funded arts project that took a lot of business away from her. She had to sell half the studio space in an effort to keep it, but eventually she had to get rid of the whole thing. It was only a few months into my first year of college when my mother broke the news to me that yet again, we would be moving. But this place would be "okay," she said.

She said.

We hopped in the car and drove back out to the countryside in Paju, over the mountains, passing by farms and the cemetery, with no streetlamps. I'm a city girl; I need my streetlamps to know I'm safe. The closer we came to the area, I realized, *Oh shit, this place is like in the middle of no-fucking-where. This is gonna be so bad.*

Again. The entire ride, my mother was trying to gas me up. All the while, I could tell she was nervous—because deep down, I knew she knew it was going to be the worst place we'd ever lived in.

We pulled up to the outside of a small, rundown church that had a red brick building to the right of it. Scattered all along the sides of the half-paved, half-dirt road were piles of litter; the stench was all around. And there my mom was, reassuringly smiling at me, as if I didn't know that whatever was behind the door of the red brick building was going to be a lot worse than I could imagine. I've lived in crazy situations since birth, but when she pointed to where our new place was, I can't even begin to describe to you what it looked like.

Back to *Parasite,* which you have to have seen in order to get this reference. You know their basement apartment that has the window at ground level and the walk-up toilet? That's called a *banjiha.* These are typical in Korea. They were built to house soldiers during the war and were illegal to live in until the 1980s housing crisis, when they were turned into apartments. This one—that I was about to move into at the age of eighteen with my family during my first year of college—makes the *banjiha* in *Parasite* look like the Ritz-Carlton.

From the outside, I could see a small horizontal window about three inches high, eye-level to the ground. My mother was still assuring me that everything was going to be okay. The entry door was so small and low. It was made of fiberglass that could easily be broken into. *Oh, hell fucking no,* I thought.

She swung open the door and—*ta-da*! The smell hit me in the face. I closed my eyes, for multiple reasons: because of the *banjiha* smell, because of what I was looking at, and because *what the fuck*?

And if you don't know the smell of a *banjiha,* it is very distinct. It sticks on you—in your hair and your clothes. No matter how much you wash your body or clean your clothes, that smell is always there. So even if you look rich, other poor people will be able to tell you're poor, just because of the way you smell. They have a saying in Korea that the only way to get rid of a *banjiha* smell is to move.

The smell just hits me in the soul. It's burned permanently into my nostrils. To this day, just thinking about the place, I can instantly recall the smell, and it still nauseates me.

I opened my eyes as we walked down about twelve steps into a short corridor, all the while my mother was trying to sell me on this place like we were taking a grand tour of some mansion. We walked down a few more concrete steps, avoiding cobwebs strewn throughout the place. The smell was too much.

Mold, bleach, and concrete all mixed in one—that's *banjiha* smell.

I saw a bucket with bleach cleaner and a rag by the wall, which became a fixture in the house. It was used to scrub off black mold daily, so we didn't die.

Now, I've been to many *banjiha,* but nothing like this one. I wouldn't even call this a *banjiha*—that's an insult to the name. This was more like a fucking mold- and insect-infested cave.

There was a small main open area with a sink, dining table, stove, and fridge. To the left were two doors, one of which led to a room with all of our boxes, clothes (all moist and wet), and two desks under which my sister, mother, and I slept. The other led to my father's own room.

And the bathroom had steps going up to the toilet. Since the sewer pipes were at street level, the toilet had to be raised above the ground for proper drainage. Behind the toilet was a huge hole that you could see through to the outside.

Not only was this in bumblefuck nowhere, in a deserted, scary-ass neighborhood, but it was also over an hour-and-a-half ride by express bus away from my college. I couldn't do this anymore. I couldn't live like this. It was too much. It wasn't just the *banjiha*. It wasn't just my father. It was everything. I knew I didn't fit in in Korea. I didn't belong here. I had one goal and one goal only: move to America after college.

I didn't want this life where people divide you into social classes based on how much money you have. I didn't want to be a part of a materialistic society that judges your worth by the value of what you wear. And I certainly didn't want to live in a place that criticizes girls for having thick thighs. No matter what my success could have been in Korea, the stench of poverty followed me around despite how convincing I was at hiding it from other people. If they weren't aware of it, I certainly was. I didn't want that anymore. Just like removing a *banjiha* smell, the only way you can escape poverty in Korea is to move. So that's what I was doing. I was getting the fuck out. I was going to move to America, be free, be me. And I had a plan.

It wasn't long after we moved to the *banjiha* that my sister finally escaped our home. She graduated; she was now an adult with a job; she got out—but I was still stuck.

Late one night before she moved away for a hotel service job she landed in Southeast Asia, we were all driving back out to the countryside to the *banjiha*. My sister had hung out with her girlfriends, and she was recounting the evening to me in the backseat. There I was, eighteen years old in my last year of high school, and she was twenty-three. We're adults talking about adult things. She tells me they had some *soju* and then a *soju* cocktail, which she never had before. She wasn't drunk; she was just a little tipsy.

Out of the blue, my father goes crazy. Banging on the steering wheel with his fists, screaming at my sister at the top of his lungs, "Shut up, you fucking bitch." When we got home, he beat the shit out of her. At twenty-three, she got the shit beaten out of her. It was never going to stop for any of us. As long as I was living anywhere near him, I would always have this shackle around my neck. We couldn't even have a simple conversation without getting the shit beaten out of us. She knew it was time to get the fuck out. That would be the last beating my sister would ever receive from my father. And it would be the last time she would ever see him again.

During that first year of college, I stayed at the *banjiha* every night. I'd leave early in the morning and go to school from 9:30 a.m. until about 5:30 p.m. In between classes and after school, I would wander around aimlessly just enjoying my freedom. It wasn't so much the freedom to walk around—it was the freedom to just be me.

I had spent my entire life lying about who I was and where I came from, how much money we had, and what my parents did for a living. Here at college, no one knew, and no one cared. Normally, I'm a bubbly, happy-go-lucky person, and I love to meet people and socialize. But during this first year, I really kept to myself. It's not that I didn't want to make friends, but I was really just enjoying this newfound freedom I had.

My mother was teaching art here and there, and working some other odd jobs to get by. She ended up landing a temporary job nannying for a rich Korean family in the United States for a few months. She would go back and forth periodically over the years. My father, on the other hand—I'm not entirely sure what he was doing. He would disappear from time to time. I didn't see him very much because I was barely home. But when I was around, and he was home, I was still cautious of how I behaved in front of him.

Oh, but what happened to Yoon-gi? The fuck you think happened; we broke up. Right after we graduated high school, he just started acting like a dick and treating me like shit. He ignored my calls and texts, lied to me about what he had been up to, and made me cry daily. And he kicked my ass to the curb. I was heartbroken, but he wanted to be free and enjoy his life because he had to join the army for two and a half years.

The irony of it is the bus I took to college every day passed by his house. It was a constant reminder, and I missed him like crazy. I consumed so much chocolate during this time trying to get over him. I didn't just lose my first boyfriend; I also lost a friend. But seriously, fuck him for treating me like that. When you show me who you truly are, trust me, I am going to believe you. And you won't change my mind ever again. I can forgive, but I will never forget.

My second and third years of college, I became way more engaged with my studies. I was enjoying studying art history and printmaking, so it actually made it fun. And I became more social; I had developed a group of art friends that I was always hanging out with. I was hardly ever back at the *banjiha*. If I wasn't staying at my friends' houses, I was staying in the printmaking classroom at my college. I always kept an extra change of clothes on me for this very purpose. All the students were so busy that it was normal to sleep in the study halls and studios. Most brought extra clothes with them and just showered in the school bathroom, which had showers for students to use. What friends didn't notice was I hardly ever went home. They did, and a lot of times, I'd go with them. I would go back home maybe twice a week to get new clothes; otherwise, I slept at school or a friend's house.

During the first three years of art school, we studied all types of art, from pointillism to lithographic printmaking. Everything.

In your final year, you get to be more creative and do what you like. In my studies over the years, I became fascinated with pop art. I studied the way they painted: Warhol, Basquiat, Haring, all the best. I read their biographies, and I really studied them and became so engrossed in who they were, what they thought, and where they were from. It was then that I knew I had to move to New York City.

All the best pop art artists were from New York City. It was a place where dreams could become a reality. That became my goal. That was my only goal. Once I finished my degree, I was moving to New York City. How this was going to happen was an insignificant detail in my mind; my focus was solely on leaving Korea and becoming a wealthy, famous artist in New York City. There wasn't anywhere else but New York City. That's it. That's what I was doing, and no one was going to stop me.

In my third year of college, I became close friends with a really rich girl who was one year older than me. She showed me how rich people live in Korea. She spent money like it was air. It fascinated me. But she was always kind to me, which was different from the way some of her friends acted. They all thought I was rich like them because they knew who my grandfather was. I was hanging with her and some of her rich friends one day when her friends started being super disrespectful about non-rich people. Just making fun of average everyday people for not having what they had. On the outside I was just listening and smiling. In my mind and soul, a lot of bad things were going on. I just wanted to punch these girls; that shit gets me so mad. No one should be treated less than human simply because they don't have money. Human is human. We all bleed the same blood. It wasn't eye-opening to me; I was well aware that rich people degrade anyone who isn't of their socio-economic status. It's just really fucking gross to see in real life.

But I kept what I was thinking all inside. By this point, I had started to act like someone I wasn't again. I tried so hard to act like a soft person, someone who hasn't gone through all the shit I have in my life. When that rage would come up in me, the feeling of wanting to punch someone would get so strong I'd stop myself and either punch the air, break shit when no one was around, or hurt myself. Not cutting or anything. Just like beating myself with my fist. I would literally beat the fuck out of myself, so I wouldn't hurt others. I held the "real" me back.

The "real" me almost came out one time because of this new student who had joined my class. He had just finished his time in the military, which is compulsory for men between eighteen and twenty-eight for two years. He acted like he was so tough and scary. But you know me; I'm not scared of a man. Especially when they are trying to act tough and scary. He didn't like me, and I didn't care. For almost a year, he was a total dick to me until one day he called me over to the staircase by our classroom to threaten me.

I usually act like a soft person until I don't want to. The guy told me he didn't like the way I acted and talked and went on and on and on. I just stood there and smiled at him. I could feel the rage coming up in me. I kept smiling because that's what I do before I lose it. In that moment, when he looked in my eyes, he knew that the soft person I was pretending to be didn't exist. He could see that fire behind my eyes. I continued smiling. He looked confused.

I could see he was really surprised by my reaction, but he kept talking. Then his tone changed from threatening to calm. And I calmed down too.

After he finished, I looked at him with that big grin on my face and asked him, "Are you done?" He didn't say anything. I flashed him a knowing smile, and I left. The "real" me got to hide for another day, and I didn't have to kick anyone's ass.

One day on my way home from class, I saw a sign for kickboxing classes at a studio near my college. You know me; I was curious. I like to punch stuff and fight, and I knew this was something I would be good at. I went upstairs and saw the instructor working out doing stretches. He noticed me and introduced himself. I said I was interested in possibly taking a class. I didn't have any money, but I was determined to do it no matter what. When I set my mind on something, I always make it happen. We chatted for a bit, and he suggested I come by sometime to take a free class. He gave me the schedule and told me to just drop by when I was ready.

I went by and took a class and, naturally, kicked ass at it. I'm not built like other Korean women, who are normally slender and petite. I am an athletic woman with thick thighs, and I'm super strong. He saw that power in me and offered to train me for free. After three months, he said I was ready to go pro. He got me a professional kickboxing license, which is highly illegal as you're supposed to run the amateur circuit for at least two years before applying for a professional license. However, this guy was one of the most respected kickboxing instructors in Korea, so he pulled some strings and got me into the professional Korean kickboxing circuit. To me, it was a legal way to fight and kick someone's ass without getting in trouble. But it wasn't about beating up people, it was about letting it all out. It was a sport to me. I'm a competitive person, so losing wasn't even an option. I ended up competing in two professional tournaments during my final year of college. You shouldn't even need to ask, but for the record, yes, I won both tournaments. Got the trophies and everything.

Meanwhile, back at the *banjiha,* things were progressively getting worse. While I tried to only stay at the *banjiha* once a week throughout the school year, during summer and winter break, I was stuck there the entire time. There were plenty of mornings where we'd wake up in three to four inches of water, not knowing where it came from. When it rained, it was even worse. The flooding of the *banjiha* wrecked so many of our things. Old photos were soaked and fell apart, and our clothes were damaged. Little by little, our belongings were slowly being destroyed.

In January of 2005, my mom came back from America and noticed our dog Mari was sick. She wouldn't eat. We spent everything we had and bought her some meat. She wouldn't eat that. My mother made some broth with the meat to see if she would drink it, but she wouldn't. We did this process for about three weeks, and I could feel myself breaking apart inside. On her last day, I held her close to me as much as I could throughout the day. Eventually, I had to go to my computer to do some schoolwork, so I gave Mari to my mom, who had been sitting on the floor next to me.

She looked up at me and said, "I think Mari just died."

I looked down and snatched her up from my mom, holding her lifeless body in my arms. She was right. We sobbed uncontrollably. She was our best little friend. If Mari wasn't with me, she was with my mom. She took her everywhere. She was the one thing that made me smile every day. She saw me at my worst, while I was getting beaten by my father, and she was there to keep me warm and safe after.

The mold had gotten to her. I felt so guilty because I hadn't been there every day to take care of her while my mother was away in America. I should have made sure she was fed and wiped down the mold every day. I just couldn't bring myself to be alone with my father in the *banjiha*. I knew he wouldn't take care of her. This killed me inside. I felt like I wanted to die myself.

I put her in a small box that night. The next day when I touched the box, it still felt warm, or at least I thought so. I wrote a letter to Mari and put it in my pocket. My mom and I ended up taking her to one of the small mountains near the *banjiha*. I started to shovel, but the ground was frozen. I pushed harder and harder into the ground, digging, crying, as deep as I could, as hard as I could, so she had a place to rest. I finally dug deep enough and put her box in the ground. I placed the letter on top of the box and made her a small Korean-style mound grave. A part of me died that day. She meant so much to me and my mom. After Mari died, I really felt like there was nothing that could hold me back. I was getting the fuck out.

At night in the *banjiha,* I would pull the blankets up over my head to cover my face to keep bugs or rats from crawling across it. Inevitably, in the middle of the night I would toss or turn, and the blanket would uncover my face. I would wake up to something touching me—you cannot imagine the horror of waking up almost every night because of bugs crawling over you, or mice and rats scurrying by, or lying in drain water. And to top it off, we had these weird spider-like hopping bugs that were jumping at us in the shower every day.

You're probably wondering how the fuck I paid for school. Like most broke people, I took out student loans. I got enough for tuition and then an additional $2,000 per semester. But that wasn't enough to cover brand new art supplies for the semester and live off. So, I usually just used that money for food and was resourceful when it came to my art. Most of the supplies I had were either found, repurposed, left behind, or discarded. That's who I am—I can use anything to make art. In order to make extra cash in between studies I would waitress at a restaurant, teach swim classes, or instruct art classes at hogwan.

My desire to move to New York City grew more each day. I just knew that once I was finished with my degree, I was out of Korea. But I couldn't wait, it was calling me. So, I decided not to wait. Between my third and fourth year of college, I took my $2,000 stipend and bought a $700 roundtrip ticket from Seoul to New York City to spend a little less than a month in the United States. That gave me $1300 to spend while I was there.

And if you're wondering—*if $2,000 wasn't enough to live off of, how could you spend it on a trip, even if your art supplies were free?*—well, it's because I'm crazy like that. I'd been figuring shit out my whole life. By then, I'd already survived about twenty-one years living that way.

Do you really think I cared?

Things were so bad that all I wanted was to run—run from a life I knew deep down wasn't even mine.

I needed this. I needed to go to New York City to get inspired to do my exit art show. I needed to learn about the pop art masters—to see it all firsthand.

In February 2006, I made the almost forty-eight-hour trip from Seoul to New York City. This was due to my cheap-ass ticket, which went from Seoul via Japan and about four other layovers before finally landing in New York City—the concrete jungle where dreams are made of. I had rented a room in an apartment, kind of like an Airbnb before Airbnb. Since I had no real spending money beyond paying for my lodging and food, I just meandered the streets of New York, same as I had done in Seoul. I was in awe of the city, knowing inside that this was where

I would be living in one year. I soaked it up. I wanted to know every street, every corner. This was going to be my city, and I needed to know every inch.

Every day, I would get up early, leave the house by 7:00 a.m., and walk from downtown to Harlem, Koreatown to the West Village. I felt like I knew the streets of New York better than most New Yorkers. I knew where to go and how to get around, but I didn't know a lick of English. My knowledge started and ended at "hello."

After a week, I started looking for work even though I was on a travel visa. Like my mom, I'm a hustler when it comes to work. I am resourceful and know how to make money when I need to. So, I went down to a new Korean restaurant on Thirty-Second Street in Koreatown to see about possibly waitressing.

This selfie was taken after I got my braids done on my first-ever trip to New York—come on, it was 2006! Taken in 2006 in New York, NY. Courtesy of Young Bae.

I walked in and talked my way into a job. I immediately started working without them knowing that I was leaving in two and a half weeks. I didn't care, because with this extra money—I could go shopping and do things in America that I hadn't been able to do so far due to lack of funds. The best thing to come out of this restaurant was meeting my friend Sera. We immediately clicked. Sera was originally from Korea but had been in the United States for a little while. Not only did she know New York City, but she also spoke English. She became my de facto translator, and we were inseparable. She took me out clubbing and just really showed me a side of New York City that I needed to see. It was so alive and vibrant. I truly felt free.

In my spare time, I would still wander around the city to look for areas I would live in once I came back next year. I was so sure this was where I wanted to be; it was like I had lived there before. It felt so comfortable; it was just right. My favorite place was Times Square, and it still is to this day.

And no one judged me for the way my body looked. I didn't get made fun of for having thick thighs. There wasn't any judgement. The only thing I ever heard was, "What's good, beautiful?" As much as I wanted to stay, I knew I had to return. I was determined to finish my degree. I had worked too hard to get to where I was to just stop.

My time had come to an end in New York City, but it wouldn't be the final time we would meet. Sera and I kept in touch. Not only would she end up becoming my best friend, but she also became my shepherd for my future return to America. I didn't have a clue how I was getting back to New York City. I didn't know how I was going to afford it. But I trusted Sera, and she had a way.

Step One: Get back to Korea.

Step Two: Finish my degree.

Step Three: Move to New York City.

As reluctant as I was to leave, it only made me more determined to get back, and nothing was going to stop me. Getting on that plane was hard—leaving behind my new friend Sera, my new city, my new life. I knew that once I landed, I would have to go back to the *banjiha* and the wet, cold, rodent- and bug-infested floor. I would have to go back to the judgment from Korean society. I would have to go back to my father.

I told myself that if I could survive the first twenty-two years in Korea, I could make it one more. And that's what I did. I focused my entire last year on my exit art show. I still slept at the school and friends' houses the majority of the time, limiting my return to the *banjiha* to as infrequently as possible.

One day, my mother said she had a surprise for me to see. Throughout my life, my mother has been known to show me surprises—which are surprising, but not in the good way. I met up with her at her studio, and she took me on a bus ride out to the countryside. I was already triggered, because you know how I feel about not being in the city. The bus dropped us off on the side of the highway in the middle of nowhere, in the middle of the night. We walked through the woods and a cemetery for about fifteen minutes, with maybe one or two streetlights along the way. Again, you know how I feel about streetlights. I need them.

Finally, we arrived at a rundown *giwajib*, these thousand-year-old Korean tiled houses. They usually have one main house, with smaller houses attached and a wall built around them. Most are so gorgeous, but this one was beat-up. I don't know how or where she finds these places, but bless her heart. She really does try.

She took me into one of the smaller side houses through a wooden door that had an electrical cord running through it into the center of the room with a work light attached to it. My mother turned it on, and it was this tiny, dilapidated space. But she was proud of it. It was her space away from my father.

The walls were just stretched, paper-like canvas over wooden frames. You could poke your finger through it and reach through to the other side. The ceiling was made of the same thing. It was warm and livable, and on the plus side we weren't sleeping in drain water. Throughout the night, I could hear rat noises. Through the moonlight, you could see them backlit while scurrying in between the walls because of the sheerness of the paper walls. I looked up, and I could see them running through the ceiling as well. They would peek their heads out tiny holes and just stare at you. Finally, I said, *Fuck it,* grabbed some clear tape, and covered all the holes in all the walls, the ceiling, everything. I lay back down on the ground, and just as I was about to drift off to sleep, I looked up, and there was a whole rat family looking down at me like, "Why you in our house?" As I drifted off to sleep, I could hear their paws sticking to the clear tape.

I spent most of my time at school or at my rich friend's house, only making appearances every so often at the *giwajib.* I barely went back to the *banjiha*—I hated that place. The smell, the bugs, the floor always wet...and my dad was there all the fucking time. My mother would tell my father she was staying in the art studio and sneak over to stay at the *giwajib* just to have a night away from him. We wanted to keep that space a secret just between my mother and me. While some of the living conditions were pretty bad at the *giwajib,* they paled in comparison to the *banjiha.* It's true we had to shower outside, use an outhouse for the bathroom, cook in the main house, and keep a rat problem under control—but we didn't have to be near my father. That was good enough for us.

One day, my mother called me up while I was at school, frantically screaming, "Your father just came to the *giwajib*! How the hell did he find it?" No secret was ever safe from my father; he always figured things out. He had his ways. It had become apparent my mother was biding her time before she finally left my father. My sister had already left, and I was only months away from leaving as well. She spent less time at the *banjiha*. She even spent less time in Korea, frequently traveling to America for nannying. Eventually, she would stop coming back—but in the meantime, my father never said anything, and neither did I. But we both knew what was coming.

Which led me to my own escape plan. I had no clue on how it was going to happen, but I had faith that it would. I had kept in touch with Sera, who had gone through a similar situation when she moved to America. She knew people who would be able to help. This sounds shady but know that I never did anything illegal. It was all legit.

While I was gearing up to finish my final exit art show, Sera and I were setting the wheels into motion for me to get the fuck out of Korea. Let me preface this by saying that it is almost impossible for non-rich kids to get a US student visa. In the application, you must prove you have enough money to pay for school and living expenses without working. You have to have full financial disclosure from your parents in regard to their assets, employment, and any ancillary documentation to prove they have the means to send you to America to learn English. If you've been following my story so far, you will understand that this was impossible.

I was recommended by Sera to contact a woman who assists Koreans who may not be so wealthy—which would normally impede them getting an American visa. I set up a meeting with her to discuss how she could help.

With a portion of the $2,000 I had received for my final semester, I put aside enough for an airline ticket—and the rest went to the woman to help me secure my visa. I sat down with her, and she asked me to explain my situation. I told her I needed to move to New York City. Then I told her about my financial situation, at which she grimaced. Then I explained who my grandfather was—a famous and wealthy man. Her eyes lit up, and she said, "This is all doable." She helped me apply and get accepted to Hunter College in New York City, studying English as a second language. That would look good when trying to get my visa.

She gave me a list of documents I needed in order to receive my visa. I compiled as much information as possible about my parents, whom this woman made look a thousand times better than they really were. But in order to really secure this visa, I needed to obtain financial records from my grandfather. I mean, we were family even though he completely cut off my mother financially when she married my father. But according to Korean law, I was legally allowed to use his finances in my application as I am a direct descendant.

The problem was getting these documents. Since we didn't have a relationship, I couldn't just outright ask him. My mother couldn't ask him either. So, the only way was to get all the information from public records and the bank. But in order to authorize access, we would need his signature—or in Korea, his personalized signature stamp. We don't sign documents in Korea; we have individualized stamps made with our signature that we use for all official documents. Getting ahold of my grandfather's stamp was nearly impossible. But creating one from scratch was easy; plenty of shops make them.

While this seems shady, I can say what happened next fully justified my actions. Remember, I just needed to attach his financial documents to get my visa application approved. I didn't need him or his actual money. He could do me this one favor in my life; he owed me that much.

I went down to the public records building and requested the necessary financial documents. When they questioned me, I told them he was really sick, and we desperately needed to get these records. After two attempts, I finally got them.

I opened the envelope. I started going through his financial documents.

Shocked—I was fucking shocked. *This motherfucker is loaded*! The number of buildings he owned all over Seoul, multiple businesses, millions of dollars. I rushed back to the *giwajib* to show my mother. "You see this shit?!" She shrugged as if she already knew all of this but didn't care.

My grandfather was known as a caring landlord. When his tenants were struggling financially, he wouldn't force them to pay rent. He would show kindness and generosity to a total stranger but not to his daughter and grandchildren. All these years, we had lived in poverty, the shittiest situations, barely scraping by—and he didn't lift a finger to help us.

I know of several times when my mother went to my grandfather's house and pleaded for help—begged him—and he refused. After my grandmother passed away in high school, my grandfather lived in a four-story house with ten rooms. My mother again asked my father if he could help us, and he turned her away. He treated us like we were less than his tenants, less than animals. Aren't we supposed to be family?

So, fuck him—but also, thanks for the financial documents.

I handed all the information to this woman, and she compiled it all together for me. I scheduled my visa interview shortly after. I went in with all of my grandfather's information, and they asked why I wanted to move to America. I said I was going to learn English. We spoke about my grandfather's career, a highlight for them. When it came to my father's information, they inquired as to why it was missing. I said he was dead. They glanced over the application and within seconds, I passed the interview. I got my fucking visa!

As soon as I got home, I booked my one-way ticket to New York City, leaving in just ten days. I had been so engrossed in my visa interview process that I wasn't aware of what had been happening in the outside world. On that very day, Seung-Hui Cho, a Korean American Virginia Tech student, opened fire on students, killing thirty-two and wounding seventeen others—making it the deadliest school shooting in US history at the time. They immediately halted student visas from Korea. The agency I was working with said that almost everybody got rejected that day. And somehow my visa had been the last one approved.

When I showcased my final art exhibition at Chugye University, it garnered a lot of interest from galleries and buyers. I was offered over $30,000 for the six-piece set. Let's not forget I was broke, needed extra money for my move to America, and would have been a fool to turn down any offer. I was living between the *giwajib,* the *banjiha,* and sleeping in the art classroom. That amount of money would get me so much: clothes, a nicer apartment, more art supplies—I mean I wouldn't have to immediately find work in America once I arrived. I could coast by for at least six to eight months without breaking a sweat.

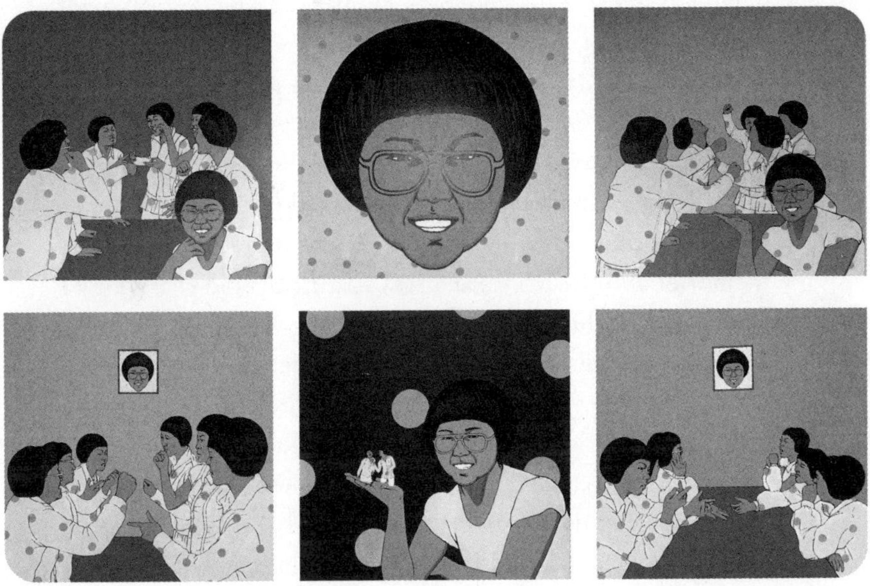

These six pieces were from my final exhibition at Chugye University—I was offered over $30,000 for them, but I turned it down because they're priceless to me. I still have them hanging up in my shop today. Created in 2006 in Seoul, South Korea. Artist: Young Bae

Yet I turned that shit down. I knew my art was worth more than what they were offering, and I refused to take the money. I felt their offer was almost like what they saw as my worth. And I was worth so much more than that. I wasn't about to let desperation for financial security be the sole reason for selling the piece. That piece is still a part of me and sits in my shop to this day.

I had already said my goodbyes in my own way. The moment I booked that ticket, I detached. My body was still in Korea, but my spirit had already left. On my final night in Korea, I slept on the ground beside my mother at the *giwajib*. You would think that I would have felt sentimental about leaving this place. I was leaving the *giwajib* that my mother had made as a refuge for us away from my father. I was leaving my home country, where all of my memories and friends were. I was leaving behind everything I ever knew in life. But hell fucking no—I was ecstatic!

Endless possibilities awaited me in America. This meant I didn't have to deal with my father ever again and never had to hide who I truly was from anyone. I could live a fully authentic life without any judgment and let go of these chains that had held me down for twenty-two years. My only sentimental emotions were about my mom. I didn't feel right about leaving her alone in Korea.

I packed as many of my belongings as I possibly could, including clothes, some photos, and all of my art supplies. I was moving to the United States with the sole intention of becoming a famous artist. I had spent the remainder of my college student loans on brand-new art supplies for my final art exhibition. These art supplies were the only ones that I had purchased—hundreds upon hundreds of dollars of new supplies that were my pride and joy. They were going to push me forward on my path to create my own name as an artist in America.

As I packed, my mother was berating me for staying out late with my kickboxing friends the night before. I hadn't completely finished packing, so while I was throwing the remaining items into my suitcases, it seemed like a golden opportunity for my mother to scold me one more time about my procrastination. This was precisely what I got, she said, for going out late the night before and not tending to my responsibilities.

Jiuen had offered to drive me to the airport that day. I agreed, but obviously I wasn't going to let her know exactly where I lived. I wasn't about to let her see the condition the *giwajib* was in, so I had her meet me near the bus stop on the highway. This was a twenty-five-minute walk through the countryside past all the grave mounds. I was lugging my suitcases all the way across this area just so she wouldn't know exactly where I lived. Yes, even at that time I still hadn't come clean with Jiuen or anybody else in my life.

There wasn't any fanfare or overt display of emotions when my mother and I said our goodbyes. It was more of a casual "see you soon." I told my mom I would email her when I arrived, and then I was out the door. As you can imagine, my suitcases were very heavy, full of paint, supplies, clothes, and other personal things. As I lugged all of this for over twenty-five minutes, I was aware of my high level of desperation to conceal where I lived. This was what I had become accustomed to doing—but this was it; this was the final time. I was no longer willing to allow this shame to be a part of my life. I promised myself that when I got to America, I would have the freedom to be me.

The closer we drove to the airport, the more my excitement grew. I looked out the window and thought about my mom—and how when I became successful, I would bring her over to be with me. All the while, Jieun spoke about how much she would miss me, how scary this must be—for me to leave Korea and everything that I had ever known in my life and not knowing the language where I was headed. It was all so frightening to her, and she couldn't imagine or understand why I was so calm about this.

But she didn't fully understand the real truth behind why I was leaving. She never knew exactly where I lived nor the conditions in those places. She never knew about my father and what he had done to my sister, my mother, and me. She didn't know about all the secrets that I had to hide in order to protect myself, her, and everyone else from the horrible truth of my reality. So, no—I wasn't scared; I was ecstatic.

When we arrived at the airport, I hadn't even thought about anything other than the immense weight that would lift off of my shoulders when I landed in America. The last thing on my mind was the weight of my luggage. When I put my bags on the scales, the attendant informed me that I was severely over the limit. I had to either pay an additional fee or remove enough items to drop the weight of my bags. Neither Jieun nor I had enough money to pay for the extra fee, so I said, *Fuck it*!

We took the bags over to the trash can, and I started sorting through my items for things I wouldn't need when I got to America. When I opened my bags, the first things I saw were my art supplies from my final exhibition. I knew these had to stay, so I started getting rid of clothes. Jieun was shocked that I chose my art supplies over my clothes. But I didn't need the clothes; I needed my supplies because I was going to America to become a famous artist. After discarding quite a bit of clothing and personal items, I took the bags and got them re-weighed. They were the perfect weight to get me to America. I gave Jieun a hug goodbye and headed through the gate. Getting to my final destination would include multiple flights, long layovers in several cities, and over forty-eight hours to get from Seoul to New York City. With eighty-three dollars in my pocket and a whole lot of faith, I was on my way to America to fulfill my destiny.

Over the speaker, we heard the announcement that we would be landing shortly in New York City. I wasn't seated near the window because I feel agitated and trapped unless I'm in the middle aisle of seats, where I feel freer. I leaned forward and looked over to my left, straining to see out the window several seats away. There it was: the sprawling New York City skyline, getting bigger as we descended into JFK. And then it hit me—I was finally home.

NEW YORK

CHAPTER 7

Fake It till You Make It

A year before I landed in America, I researched a room in West New York across the Hudson River in New Jersey, right on the other side of the Lincoln Tunnel from Manhattan. I also found the easiest and cheapest way to get to the apartment from JFK Airport as well as all the other potential information an expatriate from Korea could ever want when moving or traveling to a foreign country.

Now, stepping off the plane in the United States for the second time, I was right back where I had been a year prior when I had visited the United States for the first time. That short trip had solidified my dream to live in the United States, and now I was finally here. I had no clue what was going to happen next, but I knew that no matter what I did, God had my back.

I gathered my bags and headed outside to a beautiful spring day in New York City. According to the instructions that I found on heykorean.com, I knew that I had to take a bus from JFK into Manhattan. I'd be dropped off at Port Authority, where I'd take another bus to the town of West New York in New Jersey. From there, I would walk the rest of the way to my new place.

I looked around JFK for signs that pointed me toward the bus that would take me into Manhattan. I tried reading the signs and looked everywhere I could to no avail. I saw a bus driver, whom I decided to ask if this was the correct bus. The only words that

I knew were "hello," "goodbye," and now "Manhattan." I walked up to the man and asked, "Manhattan?" The man couldn't understand my accent and looked extremely puzzled. I thought it was obvious what I was asking, so I kept saying Manhattan over and over. The guy still just looked confused. Then I began listening around me to all the different people speaking English, not understanding anything that they were saying. But I did hear the word "Manhattan," and it clicked! I had been pronouncing it with a Korean accent, saying "Maenhaeteun." It sounded like a completely different word.

As I made the connection, I turned to the man and said with my best possible American accent, "Man-hat-tan!" The man smiled and nodded at me. So, I got on the bus, paid my fare, sat in my seat, and was on my way to Port Authority.

As we drove over the bridge into the city, I soaked up the sight of the buildings in the beautiful skyline, the artistic beauty of this concrete jungle. My excitement even surpassed my jetlag. I was elated that I was finally where I needed to be.

I listened as the bus driver made announcements for the various bus stops in Manhattan, anxiously waiting to hear the words "Port Authority." Something clicked in my head, and I realized I was probably listening for the Korean version of what "Port Authority" sounded like. I started listening to conversations on the bus, and I heard another passenger say "Port Authority" with an American accent. I filed this away until the bus driver made an announcement that Port Authority would be the next stop. There, I got off and followed the directions I'd carefully mapped out prior to leaving. I knew where I had to go in order to get to my next bus that would take me to West New York. It was a little Hispanic shuttle bus that took me from Manhattan to New Jersey.

While I waited for my bus to arrive to take me to New Jersey, I meandered around the streets for a little bit. I took it all in and felt like part of this living and breathing city of art. That's when it all felt real—*I'm living in New York Fucking City.*

I hopped on my bus and paid the fare, knowing this was the last leg of my journey before I got to my final destination. After getting off at my stop in West New York, I marveled at my environment, the place where I was going to live; this was where my new life would begin. I walked down the street from the bus stop to my house and stood in front of it, gazing up at the building and in complete awe of what lay before me. I had previously contacted my landlord via email and paid my $400 rent that would get me through to the end of the month. She had given me instructions on how to find the key and get inside the apartment.

When I got upstairs and opened the door to my room, it was better than I had imagined. Anyone else might have looked at this small-ass room—the smallest of the three rooms that were rented on my floor—and found it lacking. But to me, it was perfect. Unlike the previous places I'd lived, this had an actual bed, a window, and wasn't in a basement. This was my first real home.

The bed was a loft with a space underneath that was used as a living area. If you sat on the edge of the bed and reached forward, you could touch the opposite wall. That is how small the room was—but to me, it was just right.

The next morning, I woke up at 6:30 a.m. ready to explore my new city and experience this whole new world for the first time. I took the bus into the city, and I made my way over to Koreatown on Thirty-Second Street. I wandered down the avenues of Manhattan, marveling at the wonders. But I also had one goal in mind for the day: find a job.

I was down to seventy-two dollars. While I had already paid for rent and other necessities to keep me afloat for the first month, after that I would no longer have any money. I had already paid for my first couple months at Hunter College, and I would be starting the following week. I grabbed a Korean newspaper that had job listings in New York City. I ran through the listings and made several calls inquiring about jobs. One of them was at a nail salon in the Fashion District.

When the salon owner asked if I had experience doing nail art, I don't believe that I lied to her when I said yes. Because I *could* do nail art; I had just never done it on actual nails before. In fact, I had never done nails in my entire life—but I was an artist, and I knew how to design and create art. This seemed like a no-brainer to me. I went down to the salon to meet with the owner and do an interview for the job. I sat and waited. As I waited, I observed all the technicians and what they did. I absorbed all the details in the process, developing my knowledge base prior to meeting this woman. She introduced herself and asked me some questions. I explained that I was there studying English as a second language at Hunter College, and I had just graduated with an art degree from Chugye University in Seoul. To Koreans, a good education means everything. She immediately hired me, and I started the next day. As I was waiting for my first customer, I was observing the various techniques the other technicians were using to apply the nails.

I faked that shit until I made it. By the end of the week, I had mastered a French tip nail. So much so, that on day seven, I began training other employees who had been there for more than six months on how to do the perfect French tip nail. That's how determined I was.

The way I look at it, you can create art with anything. To me, nails were just a new medium that I learned. I became highly skilled at the different styles of nail application techniques and highly sought-after for the designs I created. One time at the nail salon, this regular customer came in to get a pedicure. At the salon, we took customers on a rotation basis. We always hated when she came in because she treated everyone like shit. Guess whose turn it was? Mine.

She sat down in my chair to get her hooves clipped and sanded down. As I began working, I made a quick comment in Korean to one of my coworkers while moving one of the lady's feet, and she kicked me. I was startled.

"Don't touch me there!"

Touch you where? On your feet—where you get a pedicure?

I went to speak but couldn't find the right English words, and she said, "Speak a fucking language, sweetie." I couldn't speak English perfectly, but I still understood what she said.

So, I cussed this bitch out in Korean. She told me to speak a language, and I figured Korean is a language, too. She may not have understood my words, but she got the gist and was taken aback.

"Where is the owner?! I need to speak with the owner immediately!"

One of my coworkers went and got the owner. She came out, and the lady yelled and screamed at her, telling her to fire me. I went to speak to explain what happened, and this lady started huffing and puffing. Before I was about to jump her ass, the owner had the lady leave. And I didn't even get fired. Well, not for that incident, at least. I did eventually get fired for my temper.

One of my other side hustles I did to make ends meet when I first moved to New York City was making chunky stone jewelry.

I saw an ad in the Korean newspaper that said they were hiring a jewelry maker. I thought to myself, *Fuck, I can do that and make some extra money each month.*

I went into the wholesale jewelry place in Koreatown on the tenth floor of this office building. The owner took me in the back and showed me how to make one of the necklaces based on a pattern they had already created. It was a test to see how quickly I could pick it up. I looked at the pattern he had made, quickly assembled a necklace, and was hired on the spot.

Every couple days, I would pick up these heavy-ass bags of stones and supplies from this shop, lug them down to the bus stop, and then bring them to my house in New Jersey. I would get home late after spending the entire day at work—either at the nail salon or serving at a restaurant—tired as hell from carrying these fucking bags all over two states. Even though I was making some money doing this, to me it wasn't art. I wasn't creating anything; I was simply following these godawful patterns. It was mindless, and I hated the way they looked. Yet I would spend late hours at home making this jewelry so I could survive.

Those first few weeks were just me getting acclimated to my new environment. Maybe by some standards I was still struggling to make ends meet, working all these jobs—but honestly, I was happy. Excited, even. Every single day of my life in New York felt unreal. Just the fact that I didn't have to worry about getting beaten up by my dad made me feel like the richest person alive. I had a room with sunlight so bright it burned my eyes when I woke up, and that alone made me feel like a millionaire.

The only thing I had to worry about was making money—and literally nothing else.

What? Is this heaven?

My thought was, *I'll either make it here, or not at all.* But the grind, much like the bags of stones, was weighing me down. I had made a vow to never be poor again, and I would do anything to make sure I didn't live like that. There was an underlying sense of paranoia that it could all fall apart at any time.

When you've been broke your entire life, and then you have a taste of what it's like to not be poor, you'll do whatever it takes to make sure you never end up in that same situation ever again. Even if that meant I had to work without sleep, I was happy to do it. I had no family to fall back on or relatives that could give me money or help in any way; I was completely by myself in a foreign country. It felt crazy, but it also made me stronger. I knew I couldn't slip or fall, because unlike for other people, that could mean death for me. That fear forced me to become more disciplined than ever.

Through it all, I knew I wasn't going to fail. I couldn't fail; that word wasn't part of my vocabulary. So I put my faith in God and myself, knowing things would soon turn around. I just didn't know when or how. When I saw that sign on that fateful winter evening, I knew it was part of the divine plan.

After about a week of settling in, I finally purchased a burner cell phone and contacted Sera, who was beyond excited to hear from me. We'd already been talking through Cyworld—a South Korean messenger app back in the early 2000s—so she knew I'd made it to the US, but actually getting to hear my voice made it all real for both of us. She became my lifeline in New York City—not just because she introduced me to different places in the city, but because she became one of my best friends to this day. I was never one to do anything that fit the status quo. No matter what, I was going to do things my way. I knew my true worth and wasn't going to let anyone tell me otherwise. I had found the perfect way for me to create art, make mad money, and live the life I had always wanted.

I would get up, go to work every day, go to school Monday through Friday, and then go out on Friday and Saturday nights with Sera to clubs. We would dress up looking mad cute in our flyest outfits, and we'd stay out until the wee hours of the morning. And then we'd stumble into Korean church on Sunday morning, still dressed in our clothes from the night before. We looked like hot messes showing our undying devotion to God.

This was something that Sera and I bonded over from day one. We both truly understood how blessed we were simply by existing through the grace of God. We made a point of going to church every Sunday regardless of what had happened the night before. That was our special time to devote ourselves to our understanding of our bond with God.

During the first year, I hadn't touched all those art supplies that I had packed away. Even after pulling a Sophie's choice at the airport, choosing my supplies over my clothes, I hadn't done any painting or drawing—which was the sole purpose of me moving to New York City. That didn't matter to me because during that first year I allowed myself to just be inspired. I didn't need to paint or draw because to me, New York City was a giant canvas. I was able to paint it with my mind and create all the potential that lay before me in this world.

After three months of attending the Hunter College ESL program, I decided to transfer to a cheaper language school, which would allow me to extend my student visa because as long as I was still in a program, I could stay in the country.

I need to preface this next part by stating that what follows is my perceived experience of what happened when I started this new school. I want to be as honest as possible without causing any issues in the future for anybody involved in a similar situation. Someone had mentioned to me that there was a cheap ESL school for foreign students. The classes were all on a pass-fail basis, and as long as you showed up to class and signed in every day, you would pass. Hardly any of the students who signed up for these courses ever stayed the entire class because they would have to leave early to go to work—either at a restaurant, nail salon, taxi, or whatever the stereotypical immigrant job was—juggling school and their job so they could remain in the United States on their student visas.

I don't know if you know what it's like as an adult—past high school and college—to learn a foreign language, but it's virtually impossible. The easiest time for a person to learn a second language is before the age of seven. Their mind is like a sponge, and they can absorb different names for things with such ease, seamlessly flowing between the different languages without any issue. But I was twenty-three, and I only knew how to say "hello," "goodbye," "Manhattan," and "Port Authority."

Many of the expatriate Koreans I had met at the nail salon or the restaurants had lived in the United States for many years, but they still could only get by with very broken, basic English. I wasn't willing to be like that.

So to further my English-speaking skills beyond the ESL school, I watched a bunch of PBS Kids shows and *Sex and the City*. That shit helped—I learned more from those shows than anything I learned in my ESL classes. Within two years, I was finally able to have conversations in English.

As a child in Korea, I watched an American English-speaking station that was broadcast for all the military personnel that were stationed around the country. I didn't understand a single word that they were saying, but I enjoyed it nonetheless. I'm certain those cartoons and TV shows in English helped me later in life as I tried to connect the pieces and understand my new language and my new home country. To this day, I am still learning English properly—and I will continue to learn until my last breath.

Me and Sera in SoHo during that era when we'd hit the clubs on Saturday and go to church on Sunday. Taken in 2007 in New York, NY. Courtesy of Sera Ahn.

I ended up juggling several jobs at Korean restaurants and nail salons as well as making jewelry. All the while, I was yearning for more from my life. I had seen many Koreans move here and become accustomed to certain jobs—which would be viewed as menial back in Korea—in order to survive in the United States. Instead of getting accustomed, I would hustle between several jobs, save up my money, and then take time off to explore around New York City. I wanted time to myself to grow, learn, and dive into the real art that was the city.

It wasn't too long after I had moved to America that my mother ended up in New Jersey for one of her nannying jobs. Surprise! But strangely, I didn't see my mother as often as I would have thought. She was busy with her nannying, and I was busy working my multiple jobs, learning English, and having a life of my own.

Periodically, we would meet up and spend time together. My mother was getting older. If you know anything about Asian culture, or Korean culture specifically, we put a very large emphasis on how we treat and respect our elders. The way you treat them will be how you will be treated later in life yourself.

While she was visiting me in New York, I noticed my perception of my mother was changing. All those things that had happened between us in Korea really didn't matter as much as they had. Sure, I still had resentment about the abuse, but the majority of that was directed towards my father—and I was not foreseeing any reconciliation with him. I was done with him even before I left Korea.

Getting close to anyone, much less a man, was hard for me. I had built up my walls for so many years as a way to protect not only who I let in but also what I let out. I had built an entire structure around my heart that was strong enough to bear the weight of all the pressure pushing down on me.

Not too long after I moved to America, I met a Korean American man whom I dated for about a year. He was born in Korea but moved to America when he was a baby, spoke perfect English, and was raised by immigrant Korean parents who only spoke Korean. For me, it was a great trade-off: he got to have a beautiful, Korean-born girlfriend, and I had someone I could practice my English with. He was decent enough, had a job, but wasn't very ambitious. He helped run his family's deli. That's not to say working for your parents' deli isn't ambitious, but he just wanted the status quo. He was the type of guy who succumbed to his mother's demands, did what his family expected him to do, and even dated a Korean girl straight from Korea—which he probably thought would make his parents proud.

Except his mom hated me. I wasn't a typical Korean woman, one who waits on her man hand and foot, honors his family, placates his demanding mother, and meets all her man's needs and desires.

On my first Thanksgiving in America, I went to his family's house for dinner and brought a pan of homemade lasagna. After spending so many years cooking for myself, I'd really learned how to hold it down in the kitchen. That lasagna? I put my heart into it—and it showed. We sat at the table, and they passed the food around. Every time something came in front of my plate, his mother would make some kind of snide remark about how I shouldn't eat this or that because I was too fat. I bit my tongue for a moment, showing a little bit of restraint. Then the lasagna came around, and her son put some on his plate.

She looked at my cooking, then back up at me, and in Korean she said, "This must be why my son is getting so fat."

Excuse me?

"Your son has been fat since he was a kid! Which is surprising because your cooking is, well, ugh."

What was I supposed to do? Sit there and take her bullshit? Fuck out of here. She was so shocked that I talked back to her, she couldn't even say anything after that. You could cut the tension in the air. Even after all that lasagna drama, when dessert came around, she told me not to eat because I was too fat.

I said, "I don't see you stopping your fat son from eating." She almost passed out from that one. So, to say she didn't like me was an understatement. I didn't care; I didn't like her either.

I had lost my virginity to him only three days before my twenty-third birthday. I had never put pressure on myself about sex; it wasn't anything I thought about. It just seemed like the natural thing to do at the moment, but truth be told, it wasn't anything to write home about. I barely remember it.

Our relationship didn't last very long after all this. It wasn't because of his shitty mother or his lack of ambition in life—although it did frustrate me. As an immigrant, you have so many obstacles in front of you: language and cultural barriers, visa restrictions, and lack of support. He had none of those issues, yet he chose to just work at his mom's deli instead of pursuing what made him happy in life, which was being a cop. He always talked about it and always had excuses on why he couldn't do it. Our relationship didn't last because I wanted a man who was self-made, someone who wanted more out of life—someone ambitious and adventurous like me. And for me it was more of a friendship kind of relationship, not love.

Just wandering the streets, broke as hell, looking cute, soaking in every second of New York. Taken in 2008 in New York, NY. Courtesy of Young Bae.

The way I look at life, every event that occurs happens for a greater purpose. At the moment, you never know what the lesson is, and some lessons you may not learn until the very end. However, I truly believe everything happens for a reason, and God will never give you more than you can handle. And if He does, that's when you surrender and allow Him to handle it for you.

With that said, I cannot explain why certain things in my life happened even to this day.

From an early age, I always knew inside that I would be a famous artist who is internationally known and well respected for my craft. It wasn't some idea I concocted as a way for me to cope with the chaos of my childhood. It was something that was true inside of me my whole life. I felt it as far back as I could remember. Along the way, I would see signs pointing me in that direction: my father bringing me back magazines from America and me becoming engrossed in fashion and American culture; scraping together every bit of money I had in college to force a trip to America, where I somehow felt right at home; always winning awards and being praised for my artwork and creativity; and coming from meager means while managing to remain humble through it all. When I look back at these moments, I know they were signs from God guiding me in the right direction. I just didn't really know it at the time.

While I was working at one of the many Korean restaurants when I first arrived, I met a very unique woman who was dining in a different section than mine. I was walking past her when she stopped me.

I looked at her, and she said, "You're so beautiful."

There was something curious about her, and she seemed to have a very kind and unique vibe to her. I could tell she was sincere.

I told her, "Thank you," but she continued.

"You really are so beautiful. I see stars around you."

I was mildly taken aback, but something in me said to listen to her. She then told me she was a psychic.

"Your aura—I sense you're going to be a star. You're going to be famous one day." She smiled at me; I smiled back, and that was that.

That short interaction stayed with me from that moment forward. She had nothing to gain from telling me anything. It was that brief—but there was a sense of knowing then, and even now, that she was right. Fame was never anything I deliberately sought; it just sort of happened and fell into my lap. But what I do know is this: if God gives me more than I can possibly bear, He will be by my side to make sure I make it through the storm.

When God calls you to your higher purpose, you'd better answer even if you're scared. Even if the odds are stacked against you, it's when you surrender and let go that He will be there to guide you along the way. And when that call comes, you'd better be ready.

In this new life I was making, I had a different understanding of who I was and what I was doing in this world. Things were starting to shift—things that could be seen as coincidences by the casual observer, but to me, they were signs. They were all around, letting me know I was on the right path towards my destiny.

Love
faith
Only God
Can Judge me

CHAPTER 8

HAPPINESS IS A BUTTERFLY

The first sign that I was in the right place at the right time came from an unexpected email. It was from none other than my ex, Yoon-gi. He told me his mother suggested he reach out to me because he simply could not focus on his studies due to being so in love with me.

Let me backtrack for a second because this needs a little bit of context. In my fourth year of college, after Yoon-gi had finished his mandatory two-and-a-half-year military service for men, he contacted me to meet up with him at a coffee shop to catch up. I agreed, not knowing what to expect from this encounter. When we met up, he apologized to me profusely for everything. He told me how much he loved me and that he missed me and how much he really needed the time away to understand how much I really meant to him. That we should get back together, and I should give him one more chance. I was in shock. I mean, this was the man I had been in love with, who had broken my heart—who I had eaten hundreds upon hundreds of chocolates to get over and cried about night after night. And he comes back out of the blue after three years and says, "Whoops, my bad, I didn't know?" The fuck out of here. It took a lot for me to walk away from him that day, but I did it anyway—and honestly, it gave me a deep sense of satisfaction. Seeing his hand shake like that? Oh yeah…that felt so damn good. I knew right then we weren't meant to be together anymore.

So, I got this email out of the blue, and it shocked me. Not because it was from Yoon-gi, but because he was begging and pleading for me to allow him to move to the United States to live with me. He said he couldn't function in his day-to-day life without me in it. I declined the offer because I left that part of me behind when I left Korea. I was in New York City to grow, learn, and move on from my past—not recreate it. That email was a definitive sign that I had to let go of what was behind me and that I was in the right place at the right time.

The second sign was an actual, physical sign. It was on a cold winter night about six months into living in New York City. I was struggling to make ends meet with my serving, nail salon jobs, and making jewelry, plus going to my ESL school every morning Monday through Friday, so I could be counted as present for attendance. The kicker was that in order to maintain my student visa, I was required to pay this school $250 a week to stay enrolled and keep working in the United States. That's $1,000 a month just for the school! On top of that, I had my rent, food, bus, and subway fare—so I had to work all these jobs to survive. Sometimes food was scarce, but I always managed to feed myself because that's what I learned to do my entire life.

One day, I was walking from my school near Penn Station to head back home to West New York. I felt this sharp pain in my stomach, and I guessed it was hunger because I hadn't eaten all day. No matter what the feeling was, I was just following my gut to where it would lead me next. I felt dizzy, hungry, and cold—because I was only wearing a jacket and little miniskirt. I may have been freezing, but I looked cute. From the outside, I didn't look like I was hungry—I was always a thick girl and looked healthy. No one knew that I was having a hard time making ends meet and that I needed extra money. As I was shivering, walking down the street, and feeling these pangs of hunger coming from my stomach, I noticed a little sign hanging from the side of a building. I could barely make out what it said, so I tried to focus my eyes on the sign, feeling even more dizzy. I could smell food wafting from inside. The cold outside and the hunger in my stomach led me to stumble into this random shop, which was nothing short of God's divine plan unfolding before me in the beautifully gritty streets of New York City. What I didn't know at that moment was the hunger from the pit of my stomach wasn't just a yearning to feed my body, but I was about to feed my soul.

There I was, standing in the freezing cold, staring up at a sign that simply read: "Tattoos."

Drawn by both curiosity and the need to warm up, I stepped inside. I climbed the stairs to the second floor and followed the signs that led me to the tattoo shop.

As I walked down the hallway, I'd already forgotten I was hungry—my curiosity and excitement had taken over, replacing it with a sharper hunger for understanding. To my left was a barbershop, and I saw this beefy, muscular Puerto Rican guy cutting hair. We locked eyes for a moment. This dude dropped everything and came out to holler at me like, "Wassup?" being all mad aggressive, but I didn't have time for that. I didn't answer and just kept walking, opened the tattoo shop door, and ignored that guy. He even followed me into the shop, but I still didn't pay him any attention. There they were—the shop owners, crowded around a pizza box, probably the source of that delicious smell. But the ache in my stomach faded as my eyes locked onto the tattoos covering every inch of the walls. The Puerto Rican guy eventually backed off and left—but that wouldn't be the last time our lives intersected.

As I stood in that tattoo shop, the first one I'd seen in my life, I stared at the neon "Tattoos" sign flashing in the window—and in that instant, I knew that this was where I needed to be.

I approached one of the tattoo artists, a biker-gang-looking white dude, and in my best, broken English I asked him, "Can you teach me how to tattoo?" He looked me up and down and said, "The owner's Korean. Let me ask him."

He went downstairs to the hat store on the first floor to get Jung, the owner. They had the hat shop below the tattoo studio, which was on the second floor, and their office up on the third. I looked at the tattoo the guy was doing and thought, *Damn, I could draw way better than that—even if I did it with my toes*! As I browsed all the typical, traditional tattoos posted all over the walls, I thought to myself, *I can do better than this easily.*

Out walks Jung, an immigrant Korean. Since I come from a family of hustlers, I can tell when someone is full of shit from a mile away—and this guy was full of shit. He told me I could come whenever I wanted to learn how to tattoo—but he wouldn't pay me for it. I could be an apprentice, cleaning up, getting supplies for them, and doing other menial tasks for free.

I said sure, and that I would see him tomorrow. And that was that. I was so excited I had completely forgotten that I was hungry. I didn't care about the pay—I was just thrilled knowing I'd soon learn how to tattoo and start making mad money. But even more than that, I could actually see myself doing this for the rest of my life. I'd been looking for something fun, something I truly liked, because I knew I wasn't going to stay stuck working at a nail salon or any of those other jobs forever. Those were always just temporary. This felt different. For the first time since I had moved to America, I found a way to make art and money at the same time. I didn't care how long it was going to take me to learn how to use all the equipment. I'm a fast learner and knew that within a few months I would get the hang of it.

The next day, after a long shift at the restaurant, I returned to the shop for my first day as an apprentice. I was determined to do this. Jung was working on a tattoo when I walked in. He saw me and instantly puffed out his chest like he was a bigshot. I walked over to look at what he was doing, and let me tell you, that rubbish needed to get thrown over the balcony like I used to do back in Seoul. That's how bad it was.

I may not have known how to use tattoo equipment yet, but I certainly knew how to draw. While art is subjective, anyone could see that this guy was just bad at drawing—and at tattooing. I didn't even know anything about tattoos back then, but the one he did looked like straight-up shit. I smiled and nodded, but in the back of my head I just thought, *That shit looks crazy.* They only wanted me around to clean up and look good. He tried to tell me about tattoos, but his words didn't hold any weight—his drawings were shit, and he clearly didn't know what he was doing. Even the barbers next door were telling me how Jung and the other artist had fucked up their tattoos. Still, I paid attention. I learned how to set up the machines and prep for a tattoo just by watching. I figured out the different needle types by cleaning the metal tubes and picked up the business side by running their errands.

I came by the shop as often as I could, and it was open practically all day, sometimes as late as 4:00 a.m., 365 days a year. I would bust my ass all day, working multiple jobs, and every free moment I had I would be at the tattoo shop watching, learning, and plotting my next move. When I asked when I'd get a chance to tattoo, Jung would just give me some whack-ass answer. He was the first Korean immigrant in America who taught me that my own kind wouldn't help me—I was on my own. So, I just continued watching him make busted-ass tattoos all the while paying attention to techniques, needle sizes, different inks, how to clean and prepare the skin, and all the nuances that go into creating tattoos.

After a few months of working for free—cleaning tattoo equipment, running errands, purchasing equipment for a tattoo shop right outside Times Square, and learning how to tattoo by myself—I was ready to do my first tattoo.

I offered my friend Kamila, a Polish woman from my ESL school, a free tattoo. We grabbed a slice of pizza, and then I took her up to the shop. She walked over to the wall, scanning through the designs, thumbing through flash books, looking for the best possible choice that spoke to her.

She made her decision. As I traced the simple design onto transfer paper, this rush came over me. I knew I was in my element. It wasn't until the reveal that I felt it inside me: *This is right. This is what I am meant to do.*

For this immigrant woman who grew up in an abusive home, dirt-poor, and was thousands of miles away from all my family and friends—to be in America, making my dreams come true in that very moment—I don't think Kamila could have picked a more serendipitous first piece for me to tattoo: a butterfly.

Kamila was my first-ever client, and this butterfly tattoo—done after a slice of pizza—changed my life forever. Taken in 2025 in New York, NY. Courtesy of Kamila Wisniewska.

It was exactly what I needed in my life; it brought about a change in me, something I had been yearning for and didn't fully comprehend, but I knew it was exactly what I was meant to do. Just like the caterpillar breaking free to spread its wings, I too had emerged from my chrysalis ready to fly.

On the bus ride home, I'd often strike up conversations with random strangers just to practice my English. But while I was working on my language skills, I was also working the hustle—turning small talk into potential clients. Yup, you read that right.

I'd spot a woman with a tattoo, start chatting her up, casually mention I was practicing my English, then suddenly "notice" her ink.

"Oh, wow, nice tattoo. You know, I'm a tattoo artist. You should come by my place sometime and get one." And guess what? It worked. After pulling that move a few more times, I realized it was time—I needed to get my own equipment. I couldn't keep borrowing from the shop forever.

During that time period, my mother had returned to New Jersey doing her nannying gig. We were catching up when she asked me if I had been working on any art. At first, I was hesitant to tell her about the tattooing because tattooing is illegal in Korea. Well, not totally illegal. You can get tattoos through a doctor because in Korea only doctors can use needles. And the people who typically have tattoos in Korea are either *jopok, kkangpae,* some kind of gangster, or ex-felon. It's generally frowned upon there. I finally built up the courage and told my mother about the tattooing, and to my surprise, she was actually super supportive. I don't know why, maybe it was because she saw the passion within me, but she decided to give me money to buy my first set of tattoo equipment.

It meant the world to me that my mother was so supportive. That not only meant she was encouraging me to follow this path, but she believed in me enough to see it as a viable way to make a living. I still cannot sufficiently express what this meant and still means to me. My heart just felt overwhelmed and full. She knew I needed money to live as an artist. She was in the struggle, too. She got it.

I must point out that I am indebted to her for her love and support. It was the first time I felt my mom really got me, and I truly felt that love. I will always be eternally grateful for this. So, thank you, Mom. I love you.

Within the first year, we had a change of ownership—from Jung to another Korean man named Min. He was stubborn as hell but seemed like a good person. At some point, Min got seriously sick and ended up in a coma in the hospital. So, I stepped up my game and ran the shop for him in his absence—unpaid, no less. While I held down the shop making sure things ran smoothly, the rest of the staff were stealing from him. They thought he was going to die, so they might as well make the most of the situation. They were stealing equipment, supplies, money from the cash register, and getting paid by clients under the table to avoid giving Min a cut for using his shop. This went on for a couple of months, and no one had a clue what was going to happen to Min. And while I was juggling it all—keeping the place afloat—dudes kept trying to holler at me like it was cute. But I wasn't there for that. I brushed them off. I was there to hustle.

The day after he finally woke up from the coma, one of the guys at the shop told me Min wanted to see me at the hospital. I went there, not knowing what to expect. He'd lost about 150 pounds and looked like a skeleton. Then he told me he had heard through the grapevine that he had lost a bunch of money while he was in the coma and that I had allowed people to steal from him. And he believed it. I tried to convince him otherwise, but it was no use. After all I did for him, this motherfucker cussed me out and blamed me for stealing from the shop. I busted my ass holding it down for him, for free, and this was how he repaid me? It's not like he could actually fire me because he wasn't paying me in the first place, but he did tell me to never show my face again.

I was pissed, but I knew the truth, and that's all that mattered. So, fuck him. It was time for me to move on anyhow.

After my fourth at-home tattoo, I decided it was time to venture out and get myself a paying job creating tattoos. Granted, I had only three nice photos of my work, but that didn't matter; *I got this.* I walked all the way down to West Village on West Fourth next to the IFC Center across from the basketball courts, where all these grungy tattoo shops were. I love walking; it clears my head and soul. The city gives me hope, and I was determined to get a job tattooing. I didn't give a shit where it was.

I entered the first tattoo shop I saw. You know me, just went right in and asked for a job. The owner looked me up and down and asked how long I had been tattooing. I said, "Three years," and she looked over my portfolio of three photos. She asked why I only had three photos, and I said my portfolio was stolen. She hired me full-time right on the spot.

You may be asking, "What?!" But she didn't need to know the truth, and to be honest, she didn't give a fuck. It was West Fourth. The place was nasty—not nearly as clean as what I was used to—and it seemed like they didn't care much about rules or regulations. But it was also pretty cool, almost like a real tattoo shop straight out of a movie. I actually liked a lot of the people I met there...aside from the pervs who tried to touch me every damn day. They even made their piercers do tattoos when the shop got really busy on the weekends. They didn't give a fuck! Now that I was employed full-time, I quit all the other jobs; no more jewelry making, no more nail salon, no more restaurants, and no more working for free at Min's tattoo shop. My life was school in the morning until noon—by this time, I had become conversational in English—and then at the tattoo shop until late into the evening.

After being in America for almost two years, I was finally making a living solely off my artistic abilities. It was the first time I was able to pay all my bills and have some money left over. I didn't have to struggle to make ends meet or to put food on my table. The only big thing I had to deal with in my life were the assholes that worked at the tattoo shop with me.

Just like at the other shop, people who came around—whether it was clients or the barbers downstairs—hit on me nonstop. The guys at the shop itself didn't really hit on me; they mostly just bullied or picked on me because I was a woman. Most of the clients I had were drunk college students from NYU plus the typical West Fourth crowds picking out random tattoos from the options on the wall or having me print stuff out on the computer to trace on transfer paper. As much as I liked tattooing, it didn't quite feel like my own art. But it was also great because I got to practice tattooing on actual people, and I was charging good money for it. After a few months of doing these template tattoos off the wall or printed from the computer, I became skilled enough to start bringing my own tattoos to life.

Then mad people started coming in and requesting me. They knew the quality of my work, and it paid off. All the guys in the shop were jealous that a woman was outperforming them. It wasn't my fault they weren't better at what they did—plus these assholes were still harassing me. So, any time one of them would make a lewd comment, try to grope me, or do any other fucked-up shit, I'd just start beating their asses. I got fired from that place twice in the span of six months because of that. But both times they hired me back because they knew I was good at what I did and needed me at the shop.

What's even more fucked up is that the one guy who sexually harassed me was never fired. They weren't even reprimanded. Instead, I got fired for defending myself—by choking them out. What was I supposed to do, let them do that to me? Hell no. Fire me all you want—I'm not allowing anyone, especially a man, to touch me without my consent in any way. Ever.

The place was so nasty, and the guys that worked there were all nasty too—but honestly, I also liked some of the people I met there, and it stayed packed, so it kind of balanced out. On busy days, we'd have six artists working at once with people lining up for tattoos like it was a sale. It got so hectic that some of the guys could sneak out without anyone noticing. That's how wild it was.

One day this older lady with a thick Spanish accent who was like sixty-five but didn't look sixty-five—big fake breasts, lots of makeup, probably a sex worker—came in and got a tattoo from one of the guys. Midway through her tattoo, I saw the guy and the old lady get up and head downstairs. I knew these guys did nasty gutter shit all the time.

A couple minutes later, they came back up and sat down in their chairs. I finished my tattoo and was headed to the bathroom in the back. When I walked past the old lady, I noticed she had cum all on the side of her head. Allegedly, they had gone downstairs, so she could give him a blowjob in the dark. He probably blew his load and had no idea where it went. She was clueless, and I wasn't saying shit. She probably did it to get a free tattoo. That's the kind of wild, nasty shit that went down in that shop—but if I'm being real, it's one of the fun memories I have from that place. I made a lot of them there.

After one of the piercers tried to grope me and I beat the shit out of him, I was fired yet again. In a male-dominated industry, this happens all too frequently. I decided it was time for me to move on and do this on my own. I'd find my own shop and create my own tattoos. I was done making crap tattoos just for money. I was proud—proud of how far I'd come, proud of the progress I was making. I started dreaming even bigger, imagining my own shop one day. The sky was the limit.

For me, *tattooing is art.*

It's my art that I create with the other person. Their body is my canvas. And I wanted to do my own thing without being harassed, groped, or talked down to because I'm a woman. Fuck them—I may have been a rookie who had only been tattooing for six months, but I'm tenacious, and when I want something, I become laser-focused on getting it.

Truth be told, I had a lot of fun working there. Sure, it was shitty at times—they tried to make me feel small, whether out of jealousy or plain old sexism—but I didn't give a fuck. To me, it felt like I was finally experiencing the real New York, both the good and the bad. And I loved it. I fucking love New York. It's my favorite place in the world.

Whenever I want to explore and get inspired, I wander around Times Square, observing everything. Most New Yorkers can't stand Times Square because it's so crowded, full of tourists meandering around, staring up at the skyscrapers, blocking everyone trying to walk past. But for me, it's magic. There are so many different cultures and people—you hear every language imaginable. There are all the lights, the beautiful architecture. It's vibrant, it's alive, and I love it. In a way, it reminds me of where I'm from—but this time, I had money to actually enjoy it. I wasn't homeless. I wasn't getting beaten up by my dad. I was finally living the life I deserved.

As I was making my way through Times Square, I stumbled upon a guy smoking outside of a building on Forty-Sixth Street between Broadway and Sixth Avenue. I looked up at the building and saw signs for a pawn shop and some bars. I stopped and asked him if he knew how much it would cost to rent a space around Times Square.

"Expensive."

"Right, but like, how much?" He flicked his cigarette and said he had a space upstairs at his pawn shop, but it was super small. I didn't care; I wanted to see it for myself. So, I followed him up the stairs to his pawn shop. He took me to the back where there was a small room, about the size of a bathroom. He said it was available for rent.

"How much?" I asked.

"Twelve hundred dollars a month."

I didn't even hesitate; I took it. I had no idea what I was doing, but I knew I needed my own shop. I needed my own shop near Times Square so I could make lots of money, do what I love, and live the life I wanted. But more than that, I wanted to create a safe space—for myself and for other people. The tattoo industry had always been so male-dominated, full of sexism and racism that made me feel uncomfortable and on edge. I just wanted to create art, meet cool people with good vibes, and build a place that was safe and happy for everyone. This was the perfect stepping stone for everything that was to come.

All I had was my tattoo gear. That's it—no chair, no table, nothing. And all the money I had was just barely enough to pay the first month's rent. That didn't matter to me because I was a master at repurposing used materials. I'd learned that throughout my entire life. Since I was little, I never had anything new.

Somehow, I always made old, raggedy shit look good. Most of the artwork I did in college was made from either used, found, or leftover supplies from other art students. Repurposing was my specialty.

I hunted around the city for random pieces of furniture left on the curb for the garbage truck to pick up at night. You won't believe it, but I ended up finding every piece I needed, including four regular chairs with wheels and a barber chair that I made into my tattoo chair. All left curbside as trash. One man's trash is someone else's treasure. I bought a MacBook for fifty dollars from some down-and-out hustler on the street—a guy with one tooth, clearly struggling. I didn't know where it came from, and I didn't care. I hauled all the pieces I could find to my new studio, tucked way in the back—you had to go through the pawn shop, then past the eyebrow threading place, just to reach it. I fixed all the furniture, bought some faux leather, reupholstered the chair, and set up my first shop: Diamond Tattoos.

I was venturing onto my own path, and it was a full leap of faith. I knew in my heart this was my calling, and I knew no matter what happened next, God had my back.

When I think back on everything that brought me there—all the tiny, seemingly random moments that somehow aligned—I realize it wasn't just about survival anymore. Tattooing had become my purpose. For the first time in my life, I felt liberated. No more pretending. No more shrinking. I had found something that made me feel seen, powerful, and unstoppable.

This wasn't just a job—it was the beginning of everything. This was New York for me.

And the truth is, ever since I came to NY, I was happy. Hopeful. People always asked me how hard it was, but I never really felt that way. No matter what New York threw at me, it was all fun and exciting to me. I didn't have to worry about anything except taking care of myself.

Maybe that's normal for most people, but it wasn't for me. I may have been living in a small room in someone else's house, but that small room was mine—and it had a fucking window. Just waking up every morning with sunlight hitting my face…how could I have a bad day?

Oh, and that Puerto Rican guy from the barbershop across from the first tattoo shop? He never gave up on hitting on me. After almost a full year of hollering at me every time I came into Min's tattoo shop, telling me in two years I was going to be his wife, that Puerto Rican guy found out I was finally single. He stopped me before I walked into the shop and said, "You're mines now." That should have been a warning, but there was sincerity in the way he said it.

All those years of building up my walls—in an instant they came crumbling down. I knew he meant what he said; I felt it. I felt right then and there he truly loved me without even saying the words. And somehow, in that moment, I knew he was right. I was his, and he was mine. It happened just like that—no questions asked. That was The Ex.

I

YOU

CHAPTER 9

To the One I Loved

The Ex saw I was ambitious and constantly on my grind. I don't think he minded it at first because that's how he was. He owned the barbershop directly across from Min's tattoo shop, raking in thousands of dollars a day. I didn't know much about him at the time, but I knew lots of people feared him. He was a short, super muscular, intimidating, dark-skinned Puerto Rican. No one fucked with him.

They were scared shitless, but not me. I could see through all of that. And he treated me like a queen. Even over the entire year that he was hollerin' at me, he still treated me with respect and like I was the most beautiful woman in the world. Don't get me wrong; he was a ho. His shop would always have these women and girls coming by to see him, and I knew what they were doing. I mean, why would I care about a man that's not mine? It didn't bother me then—I had my own thing going for me. I was learning how to speak English, how to tattoo, and running from job to job making that coin, so I could get what I wanted out of life.

We couldn't have been any more opposite, but opposites attract I suppose. While we were both deeply passionate people, we were passionate about different things and showed it in different ways. I was passionate about art, tattooing, and fashion. He was passionate about money, sex, and well, me. He only loved me. He only spent money on me. For the first time in my life, it was all about me. He was the quintessential stereotype of a Nuyorican; everything was over the top: his undying love for me, the pedestal he put me on, how he would die for me. And to be honest, I think he really meant all of that, including the dying part. If he ever heard of somebody messing with me, he would be right there within minutes and ready to kill. Literally.

We never dated per se; we were just together. It was us against the world, or so it seemed. When you have that kind of love, you tend to have blinders on that block out all the shit you should have seen coming. For once in my life, a man made me feel special in a way no other human ever had. I'm an independent woman who doesn't need a man to make her complete, but I'm not about to turn down expensive dinners, opulent gifts, and being showered with praise and love. His love was so sweet; it was like swimming in a pool of love every day of my life when I was with him. And I never asked for any of it. It was just given to me, and that made me feel so loved and protected

I always felt safe around him. Everyone was so scared, but he never made me feel that way. I had been through enough shit in my life that nothing scared me, and I knew he would never physically hurt me; it was an unspoken understanding between us. It wasn't just his size or strength that made me feel protected. It was the way he cared for me. The way he looked at me—so tender, so genuinely concerned about everything I did. That's what real masculinity looks like. He's the one who taught me how a real man treats his woman: soft and sweet, but only for her. It amazed me. Made me realize that only weak, insecure men feel the need to act rough and tough with the women they claim to love. He protected me. He protected my heart. And I protected his.

We rarely got into arguments, but when we did, it was because of drama with his kids' mother and all these hos who were still after him. So, I would talk shit, and he would just calm me down and make sure I knew that I was his one and only love. He would rarely talk back; he actually kept me calm. It was all this caring, doting, loving passion that really brought down my walls. And once they were down, I had nothing left to fear, so I was ride or die.

He encouraged me to go down to West Fourth Street to get a job at one of the tattoo shops down there after Min kicked my ass to the curb. He was there when I got my first shop in Times Square, a few blocks away from his barbershop. He honestly didn't want me to work; he wanted to take care of me, but I made it clear from the beginning that I wanted to be able to take care of myself. I had my own dreams and goals, and he supported that.

That doesn't mean the surprises stopped. In fact, he treated me like a queen throughout the entire relationship. He would stop by my shop in the middle of the day and bring me flowers, some lunch, or a snack and make sure nobody fucked with my cute ass. He would give me a rose every day. He was so sweet, always doing something for me. In July of the first year we started dating, he surprised me in the middle of the workday by taking me to the Louis Vuitton store on Fifth Avenue.

Now, you know I love my labels. Growing up in Korea, I never had that kind of stuff—I used to envy the girls walking around with their Louis and Fendi bags, name-brand shoes, all of it. Back then, those labels felt like proof that you'd made it. I told myself I'd get there one day, and I did. But now I know: the real win wasn't the stuff. It was everything I had to go through to earn it.

We walked into this five-story flagship Louis Vuitton store, browsing the aisles at everything. He took his time on each level and asked what I liked the most. I pointed at just about everything. This purse. Those shoes. That bag. These other bags. I had no idea what we were doing there, but I felt so alive running all over the store gawking at everything. He told me he wanted to know what I liked, so one day he could get me something. You know me, I told him I wanted everything.

For my twenty-fifth birthday, he surprised me with a nighttime private cruise around New York City. It was just us with the city lights shimmering in the background. I felt loved, I felt love, I was in love with him. He made me feel a way no one could; he just knew me inside and out. A server came out with champagne, and we toasted to my birthday and our love. Then he said, "I got something for you."

One of the workers on the boat came out with a birthday cake with a childhood photo of me on it. I asked, "Where did you get this?" He said he got it from my drawer one day when I wasn't looking, so he could surprise me. I didn't think anything could top this already magical moment, but I was wrong.

Then out came a present, and another, and another, and another—so many gift boxes. I opened one of the boxes, and it was the Louis Vuitton bag I had selected. I screamed. He said, "Hold on, open the rest." My mouth dropped once I realized what was in the rest of the boxes—THEY WERE ALL LOUIS VUITTON! It was every single thing I had said I liked in the store the day before.

When he took me to the Louis Vuitton store three months before my birthday, he remembered everything I had picked out. AND HE BOUGHT IT ALL. Like, all of it. Everything I pointed out to him, he ended up purchasing. He made sure I never had a want that wasn't met or a need that wasn't fulfilled. He took care of me. And I loved him for that. And I wanted to be so successful, so I could do the same for him.

Everything was passion for him, from the way he treated me and spoke to me, to the way he touched me. And the sex—the sex was the best ever. We would fuck anywhere and everywhere we could multiple times a day. Like Janet said, anytime and anyplace—we didn't care who was around. We couldn't get enough of each other. He knew every inch of my body, how it worked, what I liked, what I disliked, and what turned me on. He always paid attention to me and my needs. On an average day, we'd have sex like two times a day, but that was the minimum. Sometimes we would fuck like ten times in a day.

Wake-up sex, shower sex, get-to-work sex, lunch-break sex, after-work sex, pre-gym sex, post-gym sex, when-we-got-home sex, after-dinner sex, and before-bed sex. Rinse and repeat. And there were times in between—we were all over each other. This happened throughout the entire relationship. He worshipped my body and loved every piece of it. He made me feel so alive and taken care of.

After two years of dating, he ended up buying a condo in West New York, this beautiful place that overlooked the Hudson. At night, we would stare out the window at the New York City skyline shining bright against the dark sky. This was what I had always wanted. The poor girl from Korea who had nothing, and now this was my life. A loving man, a beautiful home, a flourishing career as an artist—a business owner making money and living in New York City. I would stare out and think to myself about how blessed I truly was. For all the fucked-up shit that happened,

I knew it had to happen to take me to where I was right there in that moment. I was happy.

We wanted to get married, but there was one little problem: he was technically still married, and she was crazy. She made me look sane—that's how crazy she was. That didn't matter to me because he made me happy. He had been with her for years way before me. They got married right before he went to prison for like seven years. He told her to leave, but nope—she proposed to him and said she'd be there for him when he was locked up and when he got out. When he got out of prison, they had two kids. He eventually left her and moved on.

The Ex was seventeen years older than me, but you wouldn't have known that. I was twenty-five, and he was forty-two, but he looked way younger than he was. He looked thirty at the most. I didn't even know his age at first, and it didn't matter to me because of the love we felt for each other. Then I found out he was married but waiting for his wife to finally sign the divorce papers. He also had two kids whom I only casually met maybe twice during our entire relationship. They weren't my kids, and she didn't want him to bring her kids around whoever he was dating—and I agreed. Plus, I had no interest in having children of my own. It wasn't a thought I even entertained in my mind.

As for the prison thing, I didn't care about his past. I didn't care that he was married, went to prison, nor that he had kids. When we were together, nothing mattered except him and me. That was it.

He never asked about my past, and I didn't tell him. He didn't know about how poor I had been, where we'd lived, about my father, any of that. And because I know what it's like to live the way he did, to feel abandoned by your family, I got that. I knew that feeling all too well. We both did. When you come from nothing and finally have something, or more than something, all that other shit is superfluous. It just didn't matter to us.

After two years of being together, in May 2011 his ex finally signed the divorce papers. When we moved into the condo together, he gave me a credit card, and I was allowed to put anything my heart desired on it. And he paid it off every month. About a week before we got married, I took that card down to Bloomingdale's and purchased this gorgeous wedding dress. On July 5, 2011, I put on that wedding dress, went downtown to Manhattan City Hall, and with only one witness, a friend of mine from ESL school, we were married.

Right after we were married, I applied for my green card, which took a few months to receive. In 2012 it finally came in, so I didn't have to continue paying that ESL school. I dropped that shit so fast. Here I was, an immigrant who came to the country with only eighty-three dollars. Now I was a resident alien, married to the love of my life, with a successful tattoo shop making art and good money, living in the best city in the world, and thousands of miles away from a life I left behind. It was more than I had dreamed of, and I knew I couldn't have gotten anywhere without God. I had weathered so many storms, and every time, I knew that God had my back.

Married life wasn't any different than when we weren't married. It was still the two of us against the world. We didn't need anything else. For all my craziness and his flaws, we really complemented each other. Where one of us lacked in any area of life, the other was strong. That was us.

For example, one day he wanted to upgrade his camera security system at the shop. He wanted to do it himself because we could save several thousand dollars on the installation. That's where I came in. He knew I was handy and smart. I was just good at everything I did with my hands, even building stuff. All I had to do was just watch somebody do it once, or if I had the time, I would just figure it out myself.

We went down to Chinatown to purchase some commercial-grade camera equipment. Now, this was one of those shops for professionals who know what to do. No instructions involved. I asked the guy at the shop casually how it all hooked up, how it worked. He showed me one time, and that was it. We went back to The Ex's shop, and I installed it. I hooked up nine cameras all over the shop in different corners and places no one would think to look. Then I had it all feed into his monitor, making backups every night to its system. I had that shit locked down like I was in the CIA.

In 2013, his father passed away. He didn't have a great relationship with him considering his father never really took care of him. When I met his father, he wasn't what I expected; he was a kind and gentle man. He only spoke Spanish, but I could see the sincerity in his eyes. He was in his sixties when he passed. While The Ex had six other siblings, he wasn't close to them. He wasn't even close to his father, but when he died, it crushed him. I could feel his pain. And from that point forward, he truly had no one else but me. Shortly after his father's passing, we sold our condo in West New York and rented a place in Washington Heights in Manhattan.

What's surprising was even my mother grew to like The Ex. From the limited times she met him over the years, she started off very suspect of him, but eventually the two of them became best friends. My other friends didn't say much about him or our relationship. Mostly because we didn't hang out as much once The Ex and I started dating and even less so once we were married. In fact, I had noticed that with just about everyone. It was like once we got together, everyone sort of fell off the face of the earth. Even the people at his shop—who rarely ever spoke to me in front of him before we started dating—stopped speaking to me altogether. Walking down the street, if someone knew The Ex, they wouldn't even look my way. It was like he had told all of them to stay away from me.

It wasn't that he told my friends to stay away, or I told them to stay away. I just didn't have time. Between my work, sex, the gym, and helping him out here and there—like writing checks, counting money, little things he couldn't do because he couldn't read or write—I had no time. All of a sudden, I realized my world had become confined to just our little bubble. I was content with that. I never saw it as anything other than us. But often when people are so blind in love, they cannot see the warning signs when they are right in front of their faces.

In hindsight, I can see all the different signs leading up to what would be the end; maybe I just didn't want to see it because I loved him so much. Maybe I didn't want to see it because I never believed he would ever hurt me.

The first sign should have been how often we fucked. No joke, I honestly cannot believe how often we had sex. In hindsight, he may have had a sex problem. I had never been in a sexual relationship other than that one time with the Korean American, but I certainly don't count that. Besides, The Ex was my husband. I just thought this was what a normal, healthy, sexual relationship looked like. I had never spoken with my mother about sex nor anyone else for that matter. It was private between us. But now I realize this should have been a red flag.

The second sign was he never wanted me to work. He wanted to take care of me and buy me things, so that I could be home for him and be his wife. Not that I would have to do all the housework or anything; he just didn't want me to work. He wanted to be the man. In the beginning, he was supportive. But as time moved on, I could tell he didn't like the attention I was getting. To him, it felt like I didn't need him anymore because I was making a name for myself in New York City. He never explicitly said it, but it felt contentious under the surface. When my business started booming in 2013, I began pulling in more money weekly than he would in a month. He didn't know that, and I wasn't about to tell him. It would have bruised his ego and hurt his pride. I kept that to myself, but he knew I was busy. I started working more than him. I started working sixteen-plus hours a day, and I wasn't able to always run away midday to have sex in his office. Or sometimes, I'd be working late doing someone's tattoo, so I'd miss our pre-gym sex. Sometimes I couldn't even make it to the gym. Simple things like that. I never feared telling him that I was making more money, but I knew how much it would hurt his feelings if he knew. So, I kept that to myself. That should have been another red flag.

The third red flag was he wanted children. Never in a million years did I want children. The thought of having children didn't even cross my mind. It was never a part of my equation, nor what I wanted in my life. He would badger me about it all the time, being pushy, talking about how "we'd have the most beautiful babies," or "I want to have a family with just you." He knew I didn't want one, and that was that.

With the kind of childhood I'd had, what kind of parent would I be? What would I have to offer a child in this world? I couldn't wrap my head around having to take care of someone other than myself or The Ex, much less a defenseless child who constantly needs your attention, love, understanding, and grace. Fuck out of here with that. It wasn't my place, and I knew it. I couldn't imagine bringing a child into the world and having them go through what I experienced. It wouldn't be fair. He didn't know about my past, so it wasn't like I could just explain all of this to him. We were enough for me. That was our family, and he knew this.

Somehow, even with taking birth control, I got pregnant twice. I took my pills religiously. I never skipped a day and never missed a dose. I had my cycle down to a science and always knew when it was coming. When I discovered I was pregnant the first time, I told The Ex. It was super early on, and I had the doctor remove it. The doctor had asked me if I had missed a pill or something. I kept telling the doctor no, it was impossible. I couldn't be pregnant, not in the least bit. We had been doing the same routine for the past several years, and never did I miss a pill. I knew my body; something was off. The Ex didn't speak to me for almost a whole month after this.

It was the second time that was the red flag. After the first abortion, I was even more diligent in taking my pills. I didn't want to get pregnant again, and I didn't want to have another abortion. And yet here I was, pregnant for a second time. When I took the pregnancy test and confirmed it with the doctor, I knew something was up. When I told The Ex I was pregnant for the second time and that I had gotten it taken care of, he was upset. I could tell he desperately wanted to have kids with me.

If I had chosen to allow myself to get pregnant, then that would have been my choice. But the choice was taken from me. I am not entirely certain how both pregnancies happened, but I knew I never consented to either one. Whether or not he sabotaged my birth control pills, neither of those pregnancies was planned—nor were they wanted. God doesn't make mistakes, but people do. That's a part of free will. And with free will comes the choice of what happens to me, my body, and my life. Besides, I was too scared to have a baby. It would be like reliving my childhood all over again. I was finally getting myself financially stable on my own. If I couldn't take care of a child on my own in New York City, which is beyond expensive, then I wasn't willing to bring one into the world. I needed to know that if The Ex left or died I would be able to take care of a child by myself, and at that time I knew I couldn't. Financially, emotionally, and physically, I wasn't ready. I also didn't want to give it up for adoption, because why go through all that, creating a whole human being and then just giving it away? Plus, there are already so many kids in foster care, orphanages, and even unwanted children living at home with their birth parents. I didn't want to contribute to that already existing pain. My decision hurt me emotionally, but I knew it was the right thing to do.

My career was moving along steadily, and business was booming to the point that I had to move to a bigger shop on Forty-Second Street and Eighth Avenue. While I was pulling in mad money doing what I loved, I was noticing something was off with The Ex. I couldn't quite put my finger on it, but I could feel it in my stomach. We were still having sex all the time, but not as often as before because I was working a lot. He still treated me like a queen, but something in my gut told me I needed to look deeper. Nothing on the outside warranted this feeling; it was just my intuition that something was off.

Because I am a woman of deep faith, I turned inward for guidance. I asked God to reveal to me what was happening and why. I did a twenty-one-day prayer and devotional fasting where you give up three things that you love the most. I gave up carbs (my rice), sugar (my sweet tooth), and shopping (my ultimate weakness). For twenty-one days, I prayed every morning, every night, and all throughout the day for God to show me why I was feeling the way I felt.

On January 14, 2015, the twenty-first day of my devotional fasting, I was sitting in my shop, working, when I felt something inside me say, *Go to The Ex's barbershop.* I stood up, closed my shop, and walked a few blocks down to his shop, in the very same building where I had met The Ex eight years prior.

I opened the barbershop door and ignored everyone as I entered his office alone. I locked the door behind me, sat down at his computer, and pulled up his camera footage.

A voice inside me said to go back twenty-four hours to 5:30 p.m. on January 13, 2015. I heard a knock on the door, and I could hear The Ex outside the office asking to be let in. I tuned that out and started watching the footage. As I watched, I could feel the blood rushing to my face and my heart beating heavily in my chest.

I fast-forwarded it a bit, and then at 6:03 p.m. on the video, I saw this bum-ass bitch walk into frame in his office. She sat down in a chair, comfortably—as if she had done this before. She knew the office and the game. I watched The Ex walk in after her, laughing. He shut the door behind them and locked it.

My heart was racing even faster. Rage was flushing my face as I saw them begin to kiss. His hands all over her. I could vaguely hear The Ex in the hallway banging on the door to be let into the office, but I tuned it out. All I could see was him kissing and touching her body the way he kissed and touched my body. His hands were caressing hers, the same way he did mine while he told me he loved me. Her panties dropped, and his head went down as he ate her out, the same exact way he did to me; the same movements, the same touches, the same everything.

The same way he did when he told me he loved me. When he told me he loved *me*. Then he spun her around and fucked her from behind, kissing her neck, whispering in her ear.

I watched it over and over. I played it again and again until it was burned into my memory—forever. I watched it ten times, and each time my heart broke just a little bit more. I could feel my world shattering with every second I watched him treat this woman the way he was supposed to love me. Every promise he made, every kiss we had, every tender moment, the life we had built together was just gone—in an instant.

My entire body, my heart, and my soul ached and burned. I had never felt so much pain in my life. Not from Yoon-gi, not from my father, no one. No man—no one—had ever hurt me the way he hurt me from watching what he did.

All the warning signs came flashing before my eyes. I felt like a fool for allowing him inside. I felt stupid for letting my guard down. And I felt hurt because in a split second, the one man who was supposed to love me unconditionally, till death do us part, crushed the very heart I had given to him. For a moment, I blacked out.

When I came to, tears were streaming down my face and rage enveloped me. I opened the door to see him standing there in the hallway. No words could ever express the seething contempt and blistering pain I felt inside.

But on the outside, I was about to show him exactly how I was feeling.

As I stood there staring at The Ex, I could see him speaking to me—but the sound was muffled. This deep shame and embarrassment washed over me as I realized there were seventeen barbers in his shop who all knew what was going on. In fact, they more than likely knew the entire time. I doubt that one woman was the first one he brought into the shop. So all those barbers knew and didn't say shit.

The pain, anger, and humiliation I felt all exploded out of me—and I unleashed the fury.

I don't really remember it all; I sort of blacked out. But from what I can remember, I grabbed anything I could get my hands on in the office and threw it. I broke it against the wall, the floor—threw it, whatever. I was like a volcano, erupting from all the pressure. I was on a warpath, and anything in my way was going to be destroyed—including The Ex. In the midst of breaking things, The Ex tried to grab my wrists to stop me from demolishing his office.

Warning: do not ever try to restrain me when I'm spinning out of control, because all my past trauma comes back to life and I go into survival mode.

And for some reason, when that happens, I go crazy—like literally crazy. When he grabbed my wrists, my brain kicked in and said, *Fight to survive*. So that's what I did. I started whaling on him, and then I blacked out again.

Once I stopped and came to, I was too hurt to even assess any of the damage I had caused. All I know is it wasn't nearly as much damage as he caused my heart.

I stormed out of the office dizzy and confused, embarrassed by what had happened. I tried to gain my composure as I barreled down the street toward my shop. I was consumed by what I had just seen in that video.

He was supposed to love me. Till death do us part, remember?

As I tried to get it out of my mind, I kept seeing the image of him fucking this other woman, some bum-ass bitch, lying to me, holding her the way he holds me, fucking her the way we made love. It kept repeating in my mind on a loop. No matter how hard I tried, I couldn't get it out of my mind. It made me sick to my stomach.

He lied to me. He broke my heart. He broke my trust. I was so confused and full of pain and rage that I had no idea what to do or to think. My mind was so consumed with what had happened.

How could he do this to me? How could he do this to us?

Although my intuition was right that something was going on, I had never in a million years thought it would be something of this magnitude. I couldn't get it out of my head. I went online and looked up our phone records to see if I could find anything. And there it was, a number I didn't recognize, dating back for over a year. I knew it was her number. The calls would be for like two hours a day—for over a year.

Out of anybody in this world, why would he hurt me like that? The man who gave me everything when I asked for nothing? The only man I ever truly loved, why?

Why, why, why? I kept asking myself over and over again. It was this emotional rollercoaster. I was going crazy. I left my shop and headed back to his, knowing he would be waiting for me. I looked at him with seething animosity.

"How the fuck could you?"

He started apologizing, saying it wasn't him. Wasn't him? I know what the fuck he looks like. I know all those moves; there was no question whether or not it was him. Did he think I was fucking stupid?

"Call the bitch!"

"Who? Baby, that wasn't me!"

"I said call the bitch. I seen her number in the phone records. Call her!"

He pulled out his phone and dialed a number, and she picked up. I could hear her voice from the receiver.

"What's up, baby?"

Baby? She calls him "baby"? I was about to jump through the phone and choke this bitch.

"Don't call me ever again. My wife knows, and I don't want to mess shit up." He hung up the phone on her and tried to apologize profusely, but I wasn't hearing shit. All I could hear was noise coming from his mouth—more lies. The trust was completely shattered. There was no going back.

CHAPTER 10

A New Beginning

I wish I could say I walked away and kicked his ass to the curb that day. Emotionally I did, but I was so confused and angry that I didn't know what to do, say, or feel. Months went by while I was deciding what to do next, but in my mind that video kept playing over and over again. It's not like catching someone cheating via a text message, phone call, or email. Those are just words. This was a video—action in motion. It played on loop constantly in my head—seared into my memory, impossible to shake no matter what I did. During that time, I lost thirty pounds in a month, and half my hair was falling out.

And to top it off, I really didn't have anyone in my life anymore because we had created this bubble that was just the two of us. My mom was on the periphery of my life. She stopped nannying around 2010, so we hadn't seen each other in a while. It felt like I had no one.

Don't get me wrong; I wasn't finished with my physical rage. There would be days where I would be minding my own business at my shop, finishing up a tattoo, when I would decide I needed to go back down to his barbershop and fuck shit up. I'm not above being messy, nor am I proud of it either. It was just how I coped with the heartbreak. After almost ten months of this anger and confusion, I packed up all his shit by myself and moved it into storage. I ended up kicking him out and kept the apartment in

Washington Heights. After about three or four months, he finally signed the divorce papers. I didn't want shit from him. What he came into the relationship with was what he left with as well. I told him the only thing he would lose in this divorce was me. That he was going to wish he had died instead of cheating on me. My love was the best thing he'd ever had. He agreed. He knew it was true.

I had never felt pain the way I did with The Ex. Throughout my life, I had become so numb to it. I was so used to being hurt that pain didn't hurt me. And then I met The Ex, and everything felt different. It was as if we had become one. We exchanged our hearts—I had his to protect, and he had mine. We somehow completed each other. And then he broke me. It was a pain I never imagined I would feel. I thought releasing my anger by destroying his shop would make me feel better. I thought kicking his ass to the curb and getting a divorce would make me feel better.

None of it did. None of it made the pain go away. I just worked through it; I literally I poured myself into my work. Often, I would have tears streaming down my face while I tattooed as memories came flooding back at the most inopportune times. I was constantly in emotional pain, but I was so focused on my art and making money that I just pushed through. No one could take that away from me. I threw myself into my tattoos. I worked up to twenty hours a day, hustling and busting my ass, making mad money just so I could take my mind off what was happening. I couldn't sleep, and all I did was work. I ended up losing thirty pounds because I just couldn't eat. I couldn't even swallow; it was too hard to even do that.

I would get to my shop at 7:00 in the morning and leave around 1:00 the next morning, pulling in a lot of money every day. Keeping busy so I didn't have to think about the pain. The building I was in was about to be torn down to be rebuilt, so I took it as a sign to make a move to a new shop—like mother, like daughter.

Now, I didn't wallow in my misery all the time. Fuck that. I started dating right away and putting myself out there. I wasn't about to let The Ex's fuckup in life fuck up the rest of my life as well. I took a few trips, too. I went to Aruba with a friend, Dominican Republic twice, and even went to Mexico by myself. I was getting my life back the way I wanted it. No one was going to stop me.

When I was searching for a new place, I wanted something smaller and more intimate—somewhere I could spend time with my clients and craft the tattoos of their dreams. I wanted it to be a place where I could create, where I could laugh, cry, just be—somewhere that felt like a part of me.

I wanted something that was my own, that was just mine.

And in November of 2015, I found it. The outside looked like a trap house, but inside the shop was exactly what I was looking for, in the perfect spot—a new location for Diamond Tattoos, right in the heart of Times Square on West Forty-First Street, between Broadway and Sixth Avenue.

It was freezing outside at the time with snow on the ground already. I carted all my shit from Forty-Sixth Street and Sixth Avenue to Forty-First Street and Broadway in the dead of winter whenever I had spare time. Lugging furniture, supplies, everything through the ice and frigid wind from one location to the next.

On New Year's Eve going from 2015 to 2016, I sat alone in my new shop looking back over the past year. I could hear the thousands of revelers celebrating the countdown outside as they watched the ball drop from the top of the building next door.

As I sat there putting together furniture, I looked around my new shop and thought about where I had come from. I reflected on my humble beginnings in Korea, moving from apartment to apartment, to the community center floor to the *banjiha* to the abandoned *giwajib*. I remembered the abuse I had suffered daily at the hands of my father, always worrying about where I would get my next meal, moving to America with only eighty-three dollars to my name and knowing zero English, and pushing and pushing myself to never give up, to get to where I was today.

Here I was on my own for the first time in a long time and by myself in America. I was a business owner with my own tattoo shop in Times Square. I had my own apartment in Washington Heights. I had clients coming from all over the place wanting tattoos from me. As hard as my year had been, I couldn't help but sit in awe of the majesty that is God in my life. Through all my ups and downs, He always came through for me—lifting me up when I was down, giving me signs and pointing me in the right direction, and even in the worst moments, never giving up on me.

I thought about my whole life and all the moments that led me to where I was that day. I knew in my heart I wanted to write a book about my life, where I came from, and what I went through. Possibly, I could give hope to people who didn't think they could make it through the tough times. I wanted to write about all of it, but who would read it? I wasn't famous, at least not yet. I mean, I had been written about in newspapers, but I was only Times Square-famous—not *famous*-famous.

I knew inside that what the lady at the restaurant said about me being famous was right, but I had no clue what the next move would be. I thought I was going to be on the TV show *Ink Master* because they were really interested in bringing me on the show.

I hadn't even thought about being on television; I just wanted to make art and do tattoos. I didn't even think TV was an option. They reached out to me three times: twice in 2014 and again at the beginning of 2016. Every time, something fell through, and I never ended up on the show.

As my business was booming, I still felt there was something else I was meant to do. So, I asked God to give me a sign. I asked God to show me what I needed to do next in order to achieve the goals and life He had set out for me. To follow my true path.

Out of the blue, I received a call from a casting director named Victoria. She said she found me by doing an internet search looking for the best tattoo artists in New York City, and my name kept popping up repeatedly. She asked if I would be willing to do a Skype interview for a spinoff reality TV show that needed new cast members for its third season, which was set to film in Chicago. She thought I would be a perfect fit and just what the show needed. We set up the Skype interview for later that week.

I had my interview with the casting director, and I didn't hold back at all. They loved me and wanted to make an offer. And then a few days later, they decided against the offer because they wanted to keep me in NYC for the original version of the show. They said they hit the jackpot with me, and I was precisely what they needed to inject life into the fifth season of the show. Within a couple months, I was handed a contract to be the newest member on this hit reality television show, and I hadn't even tried to land it. I was just myself. I asked God for a sign, and He delivered.

Sometimes the greatest gifts in life come when you least expect them, and especially when you aren't even looking. It's funny—I had never looked for TV, but TV was looking for me.

EPILOGUE

A couple of years after being on TV, I was checking my direct messages on Instagram and saw a message from some lady who looked somewhat familiar. Most of the direct messages on Instagram are from random people asking me when I'm coming to their city, so I can tattoo them, paying compliments about my tattoos, talking about the show, or more often than not, nasty dudes trying to holler at me. "Yo, when am I gonna get a piece of that?" Fuck out of here. Deleted.

I opened the message from the woman, and you wouldn't believe who it was. Remember that lady from the nail salon, the one who talked down to me and tried to get me fired, who I then cussed out in Korean? Yeah, the message was from her. She told me how proud she was of my success and that she always thought I was beautiful. She wished me the best of luck, and that was pretty much it. I paused for a moment and thought back to that day—how she made me feel, what I was going through at that time in my life—and I just let it go.

I messaged her back and thanked her. That was it on my part because I had moved on a long time ago. Then she messaged me back and suggested we catch up and hang out. *Catch up and hang out...? With somebody I don't even know? Is this bitch crazy?? Bitch, I don't even know your name—fuck are you talking about? Fuck that shit.* Having a grudge or holding onto my anger toward her serves me no purpose, but at the same time, I don't have time for fake people. In the original moment, I was hurt, pissed, and ultimately felt she viewed me as less than. I unleashed my rage at that time, but then I moved on.

That goes for everything in my life. The moment serves one purpose only, and that is to learn. If I held onto every negative thing that happened to me and never grew from them, then I would be holed up in my own internal prison of resentment. Once I let go and move on, it doesn't mean I forget. I'm quick to forgive, but I don't forget anything. That's not because I'm a bitter person—it's because that is the only way you can really mature yourself and your soul. The memory serves as a means to recall the event and how you moved past it. If something similar happens again in your life, you'll know how to deal with it in a better way.

Exacting revenge or holding onto bitter feelings is like drinking poison and expecting the other person to die. Life doesn't work that way. Besides, karma has my back. The way that lady spoke to me at the nail salon made me feel less than a human being, like an animal, like I wasn't worth anything. But that was back then, and here she was years later praising my success and kissing my ass. Karma has a way of dealing with people who have done me dirty in the past. Remember Jung from the first tattoo shop that I worked at for free, the one who thought I let people steal from him? He showed up at my Diamond Tattoos shop in Times Square asking if I had any positions available. Even after all he put me through, never giving me the time of day to actually help me out, and talking shit about me behind my back, I wasn't seeking vindication. I politely smiled and said, "Oh no, you're looking for work? That's so sad. Unfortunately, no, I don't have any positions available, but good luck out there." Him coming to me and begging for a job was karma's way of acknowledging to me, "I got you." My lesson was that no one can judge me; no one has the right to say I am anything but me. My lesson was to know that I am worth so much more. Karma showed them that they were wrong about me. Who knows, it's not my journey or responsibility to understand what others learned from those past interactions. And frankly, I couldn't give a shit less.

I can easily forgive people for their past mistakes. We are all fallible humans on this fantastic voyage together called life. It would do me a huge disservice to carry forward any negative emotion that would inhibit me from being the best version of myself, the one that God intended. But I will never forget because those memories prevent me from making the same mistakes twice or allowing anyone to treat me poorly. I know that I am better now than in those past moments. That is a blessing.

Much like art, a part of me flows through all the lines in this book. It is the recontextualization of my reality. My whole life is one giant piece of art created by God and me. If you dissect it for the individual parts, you aren't able to see the entire picture—you just see the pieces of fabric woven tightly together. Once you take a step back, the entirety becomes this beautiful, intricate, and ornate design that is the tapestry of my life.

Every day I choose to see the world in a new way for the magnificence it is. There will always be ups and downs, challenges, misunderstandings, and unfavorable circumstances, but those don't define you. Those things only serve the purpose of better understanding the beauty of your world.

Tattooing has become the closest thing I have found to allow me to continue manifesting the way I see the world. The body is a walking canvas, my artistry is a mode in which the other person expresses themselves, and we together recontextualize their experience. That is what art has always been to me—a way in which we interpret the world around us.

My story has barely begun; it unfolds before me each day through the grace of God. And every day, I know, I am truly blessed. Much like how a tattoo is an expression of self, I genuinely hope my story—and my truth—gives anyone who reads this the courage to reexamine their own life. I hope it gives them the opportunity to look at it from a different perspective and see all its exquisiteness. Through all the good, bad, ugly, and beauty, know that you too are blessed simply by existing—simply by being you.

ACKNOWLEDGMENTS

To all my clients and fans—thank you for supporting me all these years. It's because of you that I keep doing what I do: creating artwork on the canvas of your body. Your trust and loyalty have pushed me through some of my darkest moments and reminded me why I started hustling in the first place. And for those of you who came here hoping for some tea on my time during Black Ink Crew—don't worry. There's still more of my story to come. We're just getting started.

To the team at Permuted Press, including the incomparable Jeremie Ruby-Strauss and Caitlin Burdette, thank you for believing in this book. To Simon & Schuster, thank you for distributing it. To Moveable Type Management and my agent, Adam Chromy, thank you for helping make my dreams a reality.

To Brandon Deyette—thank you for giving shape and voice to my story. I spoke the words, but you carried them onto the page. You captured not only what I said, but what I felt, and you crafted it with care, even though my world and heritage are not your own. I am deeply indebted to you for bringing my truth to life.

As I've grown older and become a mother myself, I've come to understand things I couldn't before. In the hardest moments of parenting, I find grace and forgiveness for the childhood I lived—especially when it comes to my own mother. I now see how hard she worked, the sacrifices she made, and the love she gave in the only way she knew how. She is the best grandmother to Niko, and watching their bond has healed something in me.

To God—thank you for never leaving me. Even in the darkest moments, when I didn't think I'd make it through, You were there. Quietly guiding me. Softly pulling me forward. Your grace has protected me in ways I'll never fully comprehend, and Your love has been the constant I never knew I needed.

And to my son, Niko. You are my reason, my mirror, and my greatest gift. You make me want to fight every single day to give you everything I never had. Your presence in my life makes everything make sense. Thank you for choosing me. I will spend the rest of my life trying to be the kind of mother you deserve.

Finally, a note to those who have known a different version of me throughout my life: my hope is that you understand why I never revealed the full truth. It was never to deceive or mislead you about who I really am. I have always been me—no matter what. But it was imperative that I lived in a recontextualized world in order to survive. That version of me was necessary. And now, it is my greater hope that by living in my truth, I can help others find the strength to live in theirs.